AF570651

COOKING THE GERMAN WAY

COOKING THE GERMAN WAY

Shelley Byfield-Riches and Alice Judd

CHARTWELL
BOOKS, INC.

This book was devised and produced by
Multimedia Publications (UK) Ltd

Editor: Jeff Groman
Production: Arnon Orbach
Design: Terry Allen

Copyright © Multimedia Publications (UK) Ltd 1985

All illustrations Copyright © Centrale Marketinggesellschaft der deutschen Agrarwirtschaft, Bonn-Bad Godesberg, 1985.

ISBN 0-89009-837-9

Published by
CHARTWELL BOOKS, INC.
A Division of **BOOK SALES, INC.**
110 Enterprise Avenue
Secaucus, New Jersey 07094

All rights reserved. No part of this book may be reproduced or transmitted in any form or by any means, electronic or mechanical, including photocopying and recording, or by any information storage retrieval system, without permission in writing from the publisher and the copyright holders.

Typeset by Keene Graphics London
Origination by D S Colour International Ltd, London
Printed in Italy by Poligrafici Calderara

Contents

Introduction

There's so much more to German cooking than dumplings and sauerkraut, delicious as they may be! Having sampled the culinary delights of Germany from the Bavarian Alps in the South to Hamburg in the North, we hope you'll enjoy preparing some of the original and imaginative recipes we have collected for you. Although some of our recipes call for authentic ingredients which are available only in specialist shops, the bulk rely on good quality fresh ingredients which you can get anywhere. It is also now possible to buy an enormous range of genuine German products in America. Look for wurst and cheeses, breads and biscuits, pickles, mustards, beers and wines.

With its geographical position right in the center of Europe, the cooking styles of Germany have always been influenced by its neighbors. In centuries past, German royalty and the aristocracy married brides from surrounding countries, who brought their own chefs with them. The influence and prestige of these chefs spread far beyond the confines of their own kitchens. Their dishes were adapted to suit home-produced fruit, vegetables and meat, and local preparation methods were absorbed and incorporated into their repertoires. The Napoleonic wars in the early nineteenth century brought more changes. As Napoleon's armies overran Europe, they introduced new culinary methods from France which were to have a great effect on German chefs, particularly those who worked in royal palaces.

Germany is a richly agricultural nation, and this has always been reflected in its menus; local availability still has its effect on the culinary styles of different German regions. In general a great deal of pork, beef and game is eaten in Germany. Very little lamb is consumed — you're more likely to find wild boar on a menu than lamb cutlets. And there are over 1500 different types of sausage to enjoy!

Cheese and sausages are eaten throughout the day, and there are hundreds of different cheeses, usually made from cows milk, and varying in taste from mild and creamy to very sharp and strong.

Breakfast in Germany usually consists of a selection of wurst, cheeses, rye breads, rolls, soft-boiled eggs and coffee. Butter and preserves would also be on the table. This breakfast is usually eaten very early in the morning, at around 6.30-7.00am. A second breakfast is taken mid-morning. This is often a sandwich made with rye bread with wurst or cheese. Lunch is the main meal of the day. A hearty casserole or stew is usual, often made with pork or beef. The evening meal is served cold and consists of more wurst and cheese with pickles, salads, breads and beer.

The diversity of German cooking is quite remarkable. In Baden, for example, food is richer than most other regions. The Black Forest, with its abundant woodland and heavily populated rivers, means that local specialities feature game such as venison, pike, trout, and include fruit dishes like Black Forest Gâteau, and fruit brandies such as Kirsch. In Baden, meat dishes are often served with noodles, demonstrating the Italian influence on the area.

Bavarians eat a lot of meat, whether it's roasted or casseroled or used to make delicious sausages! Dumplings both savory and sweet are a local specialty. Bavarian beer is world renowned — it is stronger than American beers and made from only hops and malt — no chemical additives are permitted. There's also a wide variety of cheeses produced from the Bavarian Alpine region.

Home cooks in the Swabian (Württemberg) region pride themselves on the *spätzle* — thin hand-made noodles, as well as stuffed and rolled meat dishes. With the concentration of vegetable growing around Stuttgart, Württemberg's capital, it's no wonder that much of Germany's sauerkraut is produced in the area.

The regions known as Hesse, Rhineland and the Palatinate share specialties such as cider and wines. Frankfurt is situated in the Hesse region with its world-famous frankfurter sausage. In the lower region of the Rhine, the potato has come into its own. Potato soup, dumplings, pancakes and patties are firmly established on menus.

In Westphalia, hearty and robust foods are the order of the day. Thick meat stews, dark pumpernickel bread and delicious smoked hams are typical of the area. In Bremen, the port and the availability of fresh seafood has influenced local diet. Fish is widely eaten throughout Germany both fresh and marinated, smoked or pickled. Between the North Sea and the Baltic, Lower Saxony is famous for its honey and marzipan, and Germany's famous *rote grütze* — red fruit dessert made with local raspberries.

We have included here a selection of recipes from each of these regions, so enjoy yourself trying them out, and we wish you *Guten Appetit*!

All the dishes in this selection of German cooking serve 4 people, unless otherwise stated in the recipe.

DENMARK
Baltic Sea
North Sea
SCHLESWIG-HOLSTEIN
Rum, Schnapps, Spratts
Kiel
Fish
Herring, Spratts, Mackerel, Eel
Marzipan
Butter, Cheese
Lübeck
Bremerhaven
Hamburg
Wheat
Bremen
Beer, Canned fish
Elbe
BUTTER
LIMBURGER
LOWER SAXONY
Weser
Aller
Beer, Liqueurs, Sausages
West Berlin
Hanover
Biscuits, Cakes, Sausages
NETHERLANDS
Westphalian Ham, Sausages, Pumpernickel, Butter, Cheese
GERMAN
DEMOCRATIC
REPUBLIC
Rhine
Dortmund
Essen
NORTH-RHINE WESTPHALIA
Düsseldorf
Kassel
Mustard
Cheese
Aachen
Cologne
Bonn
HESSE
BELGIUM
Pickles, Beer, Bread
Koblenz
Wine, Beer, Frankfurters, Pickles
Coburg
Wine, Liqueurs
Mosel
Frankfurt
Mainz
Wine
Main
LUXEMBOURG
Würzburg
CZECHOSLOVAKIA
RHINELAND-PALATINATE
Biscuits
Asparagus
SAARLAND
Wine
Neckar
Beer, Biscuits
Nuremberg
Saarbrücken
BAVARIA
Wheat
Danube
FRANCE
Stuttgart
Hops
Ham, Cheese
BADEN-WÜRTTEMBERG
Sauerkraut
Beer, Spirits
Rhine
Fruit juices
Hops
Munich
Cheese
Wine
Spirits
Lake Constance
The Alps
SWITZERLAND
AUSTRIA

1

Soups and Starters

Traditional and modern recipes from Germany for warming winter soups, light summer hors d'oeuvres, and first courses for any time of the year.

Simple Cheese Soup

- 2 onions
- 1 leek
- 5 tablespoons butter
- 2 tablespoons flour
- 2 pints cold chicken stock (from a cube)
- ½lb processed cheese, cubed
- grated nutmeg
- white pepper
- 4 slices white bread, toasted
- croûtons for garnishing
- parsley for garnishing

Cut the onions and leek into rings and fry in 3 tablespoons of the butter until golden brown. Add the flour, combine well and cook through. Add the stock, bring to the boil and simmer for a further 20 minutes, stirring occasionally, until vegetables are cooked. Add the processed cheese, stirring until it has melted, and season to taste with nutmeg and pepper. Dice the toasted bread and fry in the remaining butter. Sprinkle the croûtons over soup and serve, garnished with parsley.

Tilsiter Soup

2oz bacon, whole piece

1 tablespoon butter

1lb mixed fresh vegetables, potatoes, celery, carrots and onions, peeled and chopped

2 pints chicken stock

pepper

2 tablespoons fresh parsley, chopped

4 slices white bread

$1\frac{1}{2}$ cups grated Tilsiter cheese

Cut the bacon into cubes and fry until lightly browned. Add the butter to the pan, and when melted stir in vegetables and cook until heated through. Add the stock, bring to the boil, cover and simmer for 15-20 minutes until the vegetables are tender. Season with pepper to taste, add the parsley and pour into four soup bowls. Place one slice of bread in each bowl and cover with grated cheese. Place under a preheated broiler or in the oven until the cheese has melted.

Berlin Chicken Soup

1 chicken, weighing about 3-4lb

3 marrow bones

salt & pepper

grated nutmeg

6 carrots

2 leeks

$\frac{1}{2}$ head of celery

$\frac{1}{2}$lb dry egg noodles

fresh parsley, chopped

Put the chicken and marrow bones into a large pot, cover generously with boiling water, add salt, bring to the boil and simmer uncovered for 1 hour. Clean vegetables and cut them up. Add them after 30 minutes and cook until tender. Cook the noodles in salted water, then drain. Remove the cooked chicken from the pot and cut the meat into bite-sized pieces, discarding the carcass. Remove the marrow bones from the pot and discard them also. Cut the noodles into pieces and return to the soup with the chicken meat. Season with pepper, salt and nutmeg to taste and sprinkle with freshly chopped parsley before serving.

Allgäu Cheese Soup with Egg

4 cups substantial meat broth

1 garlic clove

4 slices white bread

1 tablespoon butter

4 eggs, fried

5oz Allgäu Emmentaler cheese, grated

1 tablespoon fresh parsley, chopped

Heat the meat broth to boiling, then remove from heat. Peel and finely chop the garlic, then spread it on the bread. Heat the butter in a pan and fry the bread slices until golden brown, transfer to warmed soup plates. Carefully slide a fried egg on to each slice and season lightly with salt. Sprinkle with cheese and pour the hot meat broth over. Garnish with parsley and serve immediately.

Sweet Heroines

1 egg, beaten

coarsely ground black pepper

2 small well chilled Camembert cheeses, halved

seasoned breadcrumbs

oil, for deep frying

toast

strawberry jelly

Mix the beaten egg with the pepper to taste and dip the Camembert halves into the egg mixture. Coat with seasoned breadcrumbs, pressing the crumbs well onto the cheeses. Chill. Coat again with egg and breadcrumbs and chill again. Heat the oil to 180°C/350°F and deep fry the Camembert portions until golden brown. Drain well. Serve hot on fresh toast, accompanied by strawberry jelly.

Creamed Spinach Soup

- 2oz butter
- 14oz frozen spinach or trimmed, washed and chopped fresh spinach
- 1 large onion, peeled and grated
- 2 pints chicken stock (from a cube)
- $1\frac{1}{2}$oz flour
- $\frac{1}{2}$ pint milk
- salt
- black pepper
- pinch of grated nutmeg
- 2 egg yolks, beaten
- croûtons for garnishing

Melt the butter in a large pan, add the spinach and cook until heated through. Add the grated onion and the stock and simmer for five minutes. Mix the flour with a few spoonfuls of the milk to make a smooth paste, then stir in the remaining milk, combining thoroughly. Add to the soup and stir until thickened. Season to taste with salt, pepper and nutmeg. Remove from the heat and stir in the beaten egg yolks. Serve garnished with crushed croûtons.

Milkmaid's Chervil Soup

2 pints meat stock (from a cube)

8 triangles of processed cheese, roughly chopped

freshly grated nutmeg

1 bunch fresh chervil

Remove and discard the chervil stalks and chop the heads. Bring the stock to the boil and add the processed cheese. Whisk until the cheese has melted. Season with freshly grated nutmeg to taste and sprinkle with chopped fresh chervil. Serve immediately.

Baked Apples with Brie

4 medium sized green eating apples

7oz Brie, diced

3 eggs

3-4 tablespoons light cream

2-3 tablespoons milk

salt & pepper

grated nutmeg

melted butter, to glaze

½ cup white wine

Cut the tops off the apples and reserve as 'lids'. Core the apples and cut out the flesh, leaving the skin intact. Cut the apple flesh into cubes, combine with the diced Brie, and refill the apple cases. Beat together the eggs, cream and milk, season with salt, pepper and nutmeg, and slowly pour into the apple cases. Place the lids on the apples and glaze with melted butter. Place in a fireproof dish, pour the white wine over and bake for about 20 minutes at 180°C/350°F until the cheese has melted.

Chervil Soup

- 1lb fresh chervil
- $1\frac{1}{2}$lb potatoes
- 3oz butter
- 2 pints meat stock
- salt
- pepper
- 1 cup natural yoghurt

Wash the chervil and pat dry. Put aside a few leaves to use as a garnish. Peel the potatoes and cut into small dice. Melt the butter, add the potatoes and chervil and cook for a few minutes, stirring all the time. Add the stock and boil for 15-20 minutes. Purée through a sieve or in a blender. Season with salt and pepper. Pour into a preheated soup tureen and stir in the yoghurt. Serve topped with the reserved chervil and serve with farmhouse bread or toast.

Potato Soup

1 lb potatoes
1-2 sticks celery
2 cups beef stock
2 cups milk
1 tablespoon butter
2 leeks, finely chopped
1 tablespoon flour
2-3 tablespoons fresh parsley
salt
freshly ground black pepper

Peel and thinly slice the potatoes, and slice the celery. Put into large pan, cover with the stock and milk and bring to the boil. Cover and cook gently for 40-45 minutes, then purée. Melt the butter in a large pan, add the leeks and cook for 4-5 minutes. Sprinkle with flour and stir over low heat until the *roux* turns nutty brown. Add puréed soup gradually, stirring well, and bring to boil. Add the parsley and season to taste with salt and pepper. Garnish with either toast, onion rings, bacon, sausages or pre-cooked vegetables.

Smooth Potato Soup

- 9oz potatoes
- 1 leek, white part only
- 8oz mushrooms
- 2oz butter
- 1 onion, peeled and finely chopped
- salt & pepper
- ½ teaspoon ground ginger
- 4 cups chicken stock (from a cube)
- 2 tablespoons fresh chervil, chopped
- 4oz light cream
- grated nutmeg

Peel and slice the potatoes, cut the leek into rings and clean and slice the mushrooms, reserving a few for garnishing. Melt the butter in a large pan, add the onion, potatoes, leek and mushrooms and add salt, pepper and ginger. Cook for about 10 minutes over a gentle heat, stirring all the time, but do not allow the vegetables to brown. Add the chicken stock and boil for about 20 minutes. Purée or blend until smooth. Add the chervil and stir in the cream. Sprinkle with nutmeg to taste. Serve, placing a few of the reserved raw mushroom slices on top of each soup bowl as a garnish.

Spring Vegetable Soup with Croûtons

serves 6-8

- 1 celery stick
- ¼ celery head
- 6oz carrots
- 6oz young green beans
- 8oz fresh peas
- 1 tomato, peeled
- 1 leek
- 1 zucchini
- ½ head Savoy cabbage
- 5oz butter
- 2 onions, peeled and chopped
- 3-4 pints vegetable stock (from a cube)
- salt & pepper
- 1 teaspoon ground coriander
- ½ French loaf
- 1 bunch fresh parsley, chopped

Chop up all the vegetables except the onions into small pieces of different shape (e.g. cubes, slices and strips), cutting the vegetables which need longer cooking into smaller pieces than the others. Melt half the butter in a large pan and fry the onions. Add the chopped vegetables and heat through for about 10 minutes over a low heat, stirring all the time. Add the stock, bring to the boil and simmer for 15 minutes; the vegetables should still be slightly firm. Season to taste with salt, pepper and ground coriander. Cut the bread into very thin slices. Heat remaining butter in skillet and fry the slices until golden brown. Serve the soup garnished with chopped parsley, accompanied by the fried bread slices.

Spring Platter

serves 6

3 cups Quark with herbs
1 cup cottage cheese
2 salad gherkins
2 hard-boiled eggs
juice of 1 lemon
salt
1 teaspoon cayenne pepper
1 lb potatoes
2 sage leaves
11 oz yellow french (Wax) beans
11 oz carrots
1 medium-sized kohlrabi
4oz broccoli
4 teaspoons oil
4oz lean ham

Mix the Quark with the cottage cheese. Chop the gherkins and eggs into small dice and combine with the cheese mixture. Season with the lemon juice, salt and cayenne pepper. Wash the potatoes well and boil in their skins with the sage until tender. Allow to cool. Clean all the remaining vegetables and cut the kohlrabi into strips. Cook the vegetables separately in salted water. When tender, drain, add one teaspoon of oil to each and shake until evenly covered. Quarter the unpeeled potatoes. Place the cheese mixture in a bowl in the middle of a large platter and arrange the vegetables and ham in groups around it.

Edam Soup

3 pints chicken stock (from a cube)

$2\frac{1}{2}$ cups Edam cheese, grated

$\frac{1}{4}$-$\frac{1}{2}$ pint white wine

black pepper

grated nutmeg

4 large slices white bread, cut into small dice

butter, for frying

2 small onions, peeled and cut into rings

4oz ham, cut into thin strips

Bring the stock to the boil in a large pan and stir in the cheese. Bring back to the boil and add the white wine. Season with pepper and nutmeg to taste. Heat some butter in a pan and fry bread cubes until golden brown. Remove, drain on absorbent paper and keep warm. Heat some more butter and fry the onions until golden brown. Combine the croûtons, ham strips and onion rings and serve on top of the soup.

Piquant Soup with Egg

serves 8

5 cups meat stock (from a cube)
4oz endive, washed
5 tablespoons heavy cream
1 egg yolk
salt & pepper
sugar
8 eggs, poached
½ bunch fresh parsley, chopped
toast, to serve

Heat the meat stock to boiling. Cut the endive leaves into strips, put them into the meat stock, add cooked vegetables, and cook for 20 minutes. Beat the cream with the egg yolk and stir into the stock. When thickened, season with pepper, salt and sugar, to taste. Pour the soup into bowls and add a poached egg and a sprinkling of parsley to each. Serve with toast.

2

Eggs and Cheese

With the huge variety of German cheeses, it's no wonder that there are a lot of ways in which the Germans use them for light lunches or suppers. Egg dishes are also popular, for eggs are considered nutritious and delicious.

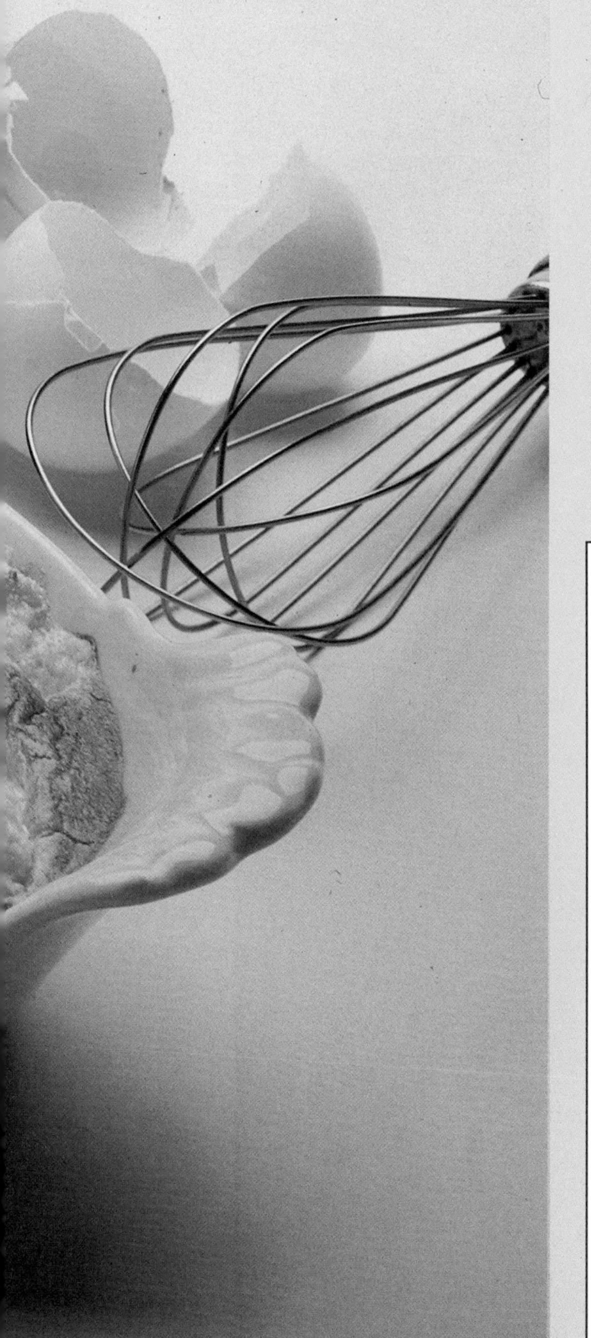

Cheese Soufflé

4 tablespoons butter

2 tablespoons grated hard cheese

3 tablespoons flour

1 cup of hot milk

$\frac{1}{2}$ teaspoon salt

pepper

4 egg yolks

6 egg whites

Preheat the oven to 200°C/400°F. Use 1 tablespoon butter to grease a 2 pint soufflé dish, sprinkle in one tablespoon of cheese. Melt the remaining butter in a large pan. Stir in flour and cook for 2 minutes over a low heat. Remove from the heat and slowly pour in the hot milk, whisking well, then season with salt and pepper and cook again stirring continuously, until the sauce is smooth and thick.

Beat in the egg yolks, one at a time, and put the mixture to one side. Beat the egg whites until stiff and fold them into the mixture, a spoonful at a time, then fold in remainder of the cheese. Put the mixture into the prepared soufflé dish and smooth the top. Put it in the oven and lower the heat to 180°C/350°F. Bake for about 25 minutes, until the soufflé has risen above the edge of the dish, and serve immediately.

Cheese Eggs

butter for greasing
5oz Allgäu Emmentaler cheese, thinly sliced
8 eggs, beaten
1 bunch fresh chives, chopped
salt
$\frac{1}{2}$ cup light cream

Grease a fireproof dish with butter and line with the cheese slices. Pour in the beaten eggs, sprinkle with chopped chives and salt and pour the cream over. Bake in an oven preheated to 220°C/425°F until the mixture is puffy and golden.

Small Camembert Pancakes

6 tablespoons flour
4 eggs
$\frac{1}{3}$ pint milk
$\frac{1}{3}$ pint light cream
1 stick butter, for frying
9oz German Camembert
ground cinnamon, for sprinkling

Mix the flour and eggs together well in a bowl. Stir in the milk and cream. Heat a little butter in a small skillet and pour in enough batter to make a thin pancake. When bubbles appear on the surface, arrange some Camembert slices on top, just off center, and fold the pancake in half. Transfer to a greased fireproof dish. Prepare more pancakes in the same way, until all the batter and cheese are used up, placing them in the ovenproof dish as they are cooked. Finally, sprinkle the pancakes with cinnamon and brown under a medium broiler.

Home Made Noodles with Emmentaler

6 eggs
salt
5 cups plain flour, sifted
2-3 tablespoons of water, as needed
1 tablespoon oil
2 cups Emmentaler cheese, grated
4 large onions, peeled and cut into rings
3oz butter

Preheat the oven to 180°C/350°F. Beat the eggs with a little salt and add the flour to form a dough, adding the water as necessary. Work the dough until it forms bubbles. Bring a pan of salted water to the boil, and add the oil. Cut the dough into thin strips with a noodle machine or by hand, and add to the boiling water. As soon as the noodles rise to the surface, remove with a slotted spoon, drain and place in a warmed fireproof dish. Sprinkle a layer of grated cheese on top and keep warm in the preheated oven. When the next batch of noodles is ready, add to the bowl, and sprinkle with more grated cheese. Carry on doing this until all the dough and cheese have been used up, then fry the onion rings in butter until golden brown, and arrange on top of the noodles just before serving.

Fluffy Spinach Soufflé

2oz butter

1 onion, peeled and chopped

1lb fresh spinach, trimmed and washed

salt

grated nutmeg

10fl oz light cream

4 eggs, separated

Grease a 2 pint soufflé dish with butter and preheat the oven to 200°C/400°F. Heat the butter in a large pan and fry the onion until transparent. Put the spinach in a little water and bring to the boil. Simmer over a low heat for about five minutes. Take off the heat, squeeze out the surplus juices and place in a mixing bowl. Season with salt and nutmeg. Beat together the cream and egg yolks and add to the spinach mixture. Whisk egg whites until stiff and fold in. Pile the prepared soufflé dish and bake for 25-30 minutes until well risen. Serve immediately.

Egg with Shrimps

12 eggs

salt & pepper

paprika, to taste

¼ cup fat bacon or German speck, cut into cubes

1 15oz tin asparagus spears, drained and chopped

1oz butter

1 7oz tin of shrimps, drained

Break the eggs into a bowl, season with salt, pepper and paprika and whisk well. Heat the bacon in a large skillet until the fat runs. Reserve a few pieces of asparagus and a few shrimps for garnishing and add the rest to the skillet, stirring gently to coat thoroughly in oil. Pour the beaten eggs into the hot pan and allow to set, stirring occasionally, over a medium heat. Garnish with the reserved shrimps and asparagus pieces, cover, and cook for 3 minutes more, before serving.

Tomato Soufflé

1 packet instant white sauce mix (to make up to 1 pint)

1 lb tomatoes

salt & pepper

pinch of sugar

4 eggs, separated

Prepare the white sauce according to the instructions on the packet. Preheat the oven to 180°C/350°F. Place the tomatoes in a bowl and cover with boiling water, leave for a few moments then carefully remove and slip off the skins. Halve the tomatoes and remove the seeds. Cut the flesh into dice, put in a pan over a low heat and season with salt, pepper and a pinch of sugar to taste. Continue cooking over a low heat until all the liquid has evaporated. Sieve the tomato pulp, bring to the boil and add the white sauce. Remove from the heat, allow to cool slightly and add the beaten egg yolks. Whisk the egg whites until stiff and fold into the tomato mixture. Pour into individual soufflé dishes and bake in the preheated oven for about 15 minutes until golden brown and puffy.

Poached Eggs with Chervil or Cress Foam

8 eggs
4 tablespoons wine vinegar
2 small onions, peeled and finely chopped
6oz butter
3oz chervil or mustard and cress, coarsely chopped
2 egg yolks
1 tablespoon lemon juice
salt
freshly ground black pepper
1 egg white
fresh herbs, for garnishing

Heat 1 inch water in a shallow pan, add the wine vinegar and bring to a gentle simmer. Poach the eggs individually for 2-3 minutes then remove with a slotted spoon and keep warm. Heat a spoonful of butter in a pan and fry the onions until transparent. Add half the chervil or cress, mix together, and leave to cool. Melt the remaining butter and allow to cool. Whisk the egg yolks with the lemon juice in a pan standing over hot water until frothy, then add melted butter, a spoonful at a time, whisking all the time. Season carefully with salt and pepper. Beat the egg white until stiff and fold into the butter mixture, along with the remaining chopped chervil or cress and the onion herb mixture. Pour the sauce into a shallow dish, place the poached eggs on top, and garnish with fresh herbs.

Golden Egg Noodles

1lb dry egg noodles

3oz butter

3 carrots, cleaned and thinly sliced

1 leek, cleaned and thinly sliced

salt & pepper

7oz tin mushrooms, drained

pinch of dried tarragon

1 cup Westphalian (smoked German) ham, cut into cubes

8 eggs, beaten

paprika

$\frac{1}{2}$ cup grated Allgäu Emmentaler cheese

Bring a pan of salted water to the boil and cook the noodles for 5-7 minutes; they should only be partly cooked. Strain and cool under lukewarm running water. Heat half the butter in a pan and par-cook the carrots and leek. Add the drained mushrooms. Season with salt, pepper and tarragon. Heat the remaining butter in another pan and add the cubed ham. When heated through add the beaten eggs and season with salt, paprika and pepper. Allow to thicken, stirring continuously. Mix the partly cooked noodles and vegetables with the scrambled egg mixture and put into a fireproof dish. Sprinkle the cheese over and put briefly under the broiler until browned.

Light 'Lüneburger' Snack

- a few lettuce leaves
- 14oz Gouda cheese, cut into strips
- 9oz cooked chicken, cut into bite-sized pieces
- ½ small cucumber, unpeeled and finely sliced
- 4-6 radishes, finely sliced
- 1 cup natural yoghurt
- 2 tablespoons lemon juice
- 1 teaspoon sugar
- pinch of salt
- pepper
- 2 tablespoons fresh parsley, finely chopped
- dill, chives, chervil — fresh, to taste
- mustard and cress, to garnish

Line a large salad bowl or individual salad bowls with lettuce leaves. Combine the cheese, chicken, cucumber and radishes and place in a salad bowl. Make a dressing by mixing together the yoghurt, lemon juice, sugar, salt, pepper and herbs and pour over the salad. Garnish with cress, and serve.

These pages: Right, **Imperial Pancakes** (*see recipe on page* 139). Below, **Farmer's Breakfast** (*see recipe on page* 109). *Below right*, **German Omelette.**

German Omelette

8 eggs

salt

freshly ground white pepper

grated nutmeg, to taste

2oz butter

1 tablespoon fresh parsley, finely chopped

Whisk the eggs together in a bowl and season with salt and white pepper. Melt the butter in a large skillet and add the eggs. Cook over low heat until just set, then add the chopped parsley and fold over. To serve, cut into wedges. Fill as liked.

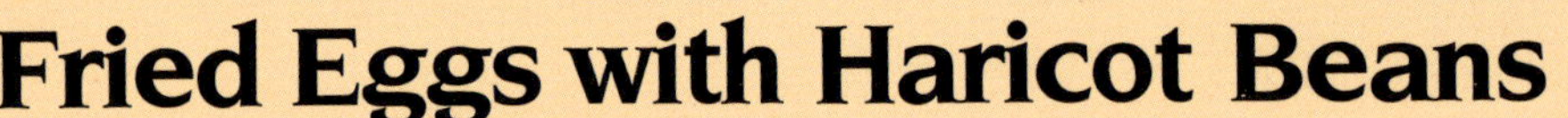

Fried Eggs with Haricot Beans

2oz butter

3 onions, peeled and cut into rings

1 bell pepper, cored, seeded and cut into strips

15oz tin haricot beans, drained

salt

white pepper

$\frac{1}{2}$-1 teaspoon dried basil, to taste

8 thin slices bacon

8 eggs

paprika

To serve:

4 slices toast

Melt half the butter in a skillet and cook the onion rings and pepper strips for 6 minutes. Add the haricot beans and season with salt, pepper and basil. Melt the remaining butter in another skillet, and slowly fry the bacon slices. Remove from the skillet and keep warm. Break the eggs into the skillet and fry gently for about 3 minutes each, then season with salt and paprika.

To serve, arrange 2 fried eggs and 2 bacon rashers on each slice of toast, surround with the beans and pepper mixture.

Cheese in Aspic

- $1\frac{1}{2}$ pints strong meat broth (fat removed)
- 12 leaves white gelatin
- 1 cup mixed pickles, drained
- 8oz Gouda cheese, cut in $\frac{1}{4}$ inch slices
- 3 hard boiled eggs, cut into strips, slices or dice
- 4 slices cured ham, cut into strips, slices or dice
- 2 tomatoes, peeled, cut into slices or dice

Prepare an aspic from the broth and the gelatin following the instructions on gelatin packet. Rinse out a 10 inch bread pan with iced water and pour a $\frac{1}{4}$ inch layer of the meat aspic into it. Leave to set. If necessary, cut the mixed pickles into pieces. Cut the Gouda cheese into shapes such as squares, triangles and circles. Layer the eggs, ham, tomatoes and cheese into the tin, covering each layer with the meat aspic as you go and leaving it to set. Finish off with a layer of meat aspic and chill until firmly set. Turn out on to a serving platter and serve cold, cut into thick slices.

Cheese and Ham Ramekin

- 8-10 slices white bread
- 8 large slices Emmentaler cheese
- 6 slices Westphalian smoked ham, diced
- 3 eggs
- 1 pint milk
- salt & pepper
- grated nutmeg

Arrange alternate slices of overlapping bread and cheese in a flan dish, then scatter the ham over. Beat together the eggs and the milk, add salt, pepper and nutmeg to taste and pour over the cheese, bread and ham. Bake in an oven preheated to 200°C/400°F for about 25 minutes, then serve immediately with a green salad.

Garnished Egg Supper

10 hard-boiled eggs

6 tablespoons mayonnaise

½ teaspoon salt

white pepper, to taste

Garnish:

gherkins

leek rings

cooked carrot slices

small bell peppers, cored, seeded and cut into strips

capers

onion rings

lumpfish roe

shrimps

rolls of sliced lox

cocktail onions

tomato slices

sardine fillets

mustard and cress

dill

Salad:

¼ head endive, washed

½ cup shrimps

1 tablespoon chopped onion

1 tablespoon vinegar

3 tablespoons olive oil

salt

white pepper

Halve the eggs lengthways, take out the yolk and press through a sieve. Combine with the mayonnaise, salt and pepper and stir until smooth. Refill the egg whites. Lay the stuffed egg halves on a large platter and arrange the garnish ingredients around them. To make the salad, shred the endive into pieces and mix with the shrimps and the chopped onion in a large bowl. Prepare a dressing from the vinegar, oil, salt and pepper and sprinkle over the salad. Serve the egg platter accompanied by the salad.

Buttered Eggs with Mushrooms

2oz butter

1 small onion, peeled and chopped

4 cups mushrooms, wiped and sliced

salt & pepper

1 tablespoon fresh parsley, chopped

butter, for greasing

4 eggs

chopped fresh parsley, to garnish

Heat half the butter in a skillet and fry the onions until translucent. Add the mushrooms and cook until soft. Season with salt and pepper, sprinkle with the parsley and divide between four buttered individual fireproof dishes. Break an egg into each dish and season with salt and pepper. Cut the remaining butter into very small pieces and add to the eggs. Cook in an oven preheated to 180°C/350°F for 15 minutes or until set. Sprinkle with chopped parsley.

Cheese Pears

4 ripe pears

½lb German mushroom Brie

1 teaspoon butter

½ 5 fl oz pot natural unflavored yoghurt

2 teaspoons fresh dill, chopped

2 teaspoons fresh parsley, chopped

salt & pepper

Cut a 'lid' off the stalk end of each pear. Scoop the flesh out with a teaspoon, leaving the skin intact, and discard the cores. Cut the flesh into cubes. Mash the mushroom cheese and butter with a fork, and combine with the yoghurt, dill, parsley and salt and pepper to taste. Fill the hollowed out pears with the mixture, replace the lids and serve, on fresh pear leaves if available.

Cheese and Egg Flan

Pastry:

- ½ cup Quark (low fat soft cheese)
- 4 tablespoons oil
- 1 egg
- 1-2 tablespoons milk
- pinch of salt
- 1½ cups plain flour, sifted
- 1 teaspoon baking powder

Filling:

- 1 cup German ham, diced
- 2 onions, peeled and chopped
- 2 tablespoons butter
- 6 eggs, beaten
- ¾ cup grated Allgäu Emmentaler cheese
- 5 tablespoons heavy cream
- ½ bunch fresh chives, chopped
- salt
- white pepper
- 4 hard-boiled eggs, halved
- tomato wedges for garnish

To make the pastry, mix the Quark, oil, egg, milk, salt, flour and baking powder to form a dough. Roll out and line the base and sides of a 9 inch spring-form cake tin and prick the base several times with a fork. Par-bake for 10 minutes in an oven preheated to 180°C/350°F.

For the filling, heat the butter in a skillet and fry the ham and onions until transparent. Allow to cool. Mix together the grated cheese, cream, chopped chives and the sautéed ham and onions and beaten eggs. Season with salt and pepper. Pour the mixture into the par-baked case and arrange the halved hard-boiled eggs in the mixture. Bake for 20-30 minutes in an oven preheated to 200°C/400°F until firm. Garnish with tomato wedges. Can be served hot or cold with green salad.

Egg and Vegetable Surprise

1 cup carrot strips

$1\frac{1}{2}$ cups celery sliced

1 cup fresh peas

2 tomatoes

1 cup cooked ham, cubed

1 oz butter

$\frac{1}{2}$ cup scallions, chopped

salt & pepper

4 eggs, beaten

1 teaspoon fresh parsley, chopped

Blanch the carrots, celery and peas in boiling salted water, then drain and keep warm. Put the tomatoes in a bowl, cover with boiling water, then remove, and slip off the skins. Halve them, remove the seeds and cut into slices. Melt the butter in a large skillet and cook the scallions over a low heat. Add the par-cooked vegetables and fry for several minutes, stirring several times. Add the tomatoes and ham and season with salt and pepper. Add the beaten eggs, stir to mix with the vegetables and cook until firm. Serve sprinkled with parsley.

Spinach Flan

12oz frozen puff pastry, thawed

2lb fresh spinach, trimmed and washed

3 cups Quark (low fat soft cheese)

4 eggs, beaten

juice of 1 lemon

salt & pepper

1 teaspoon dried oregano

6oz fat bacon or German speck, diced

4 eggs, whole

1 pot unsweetened lemon flavored yoghurt

Roll out puff pastry and line the base and sides of an 8 inch diameter loose-bottomed flan tin. Cook the spinach in a covered pan for 5-10 minutes until soft, and drain well. Mix the Quark with the beaten eggs and lemon juice, season with salt and pepper and add the oregano. Fold in the bacon or speck. Mix the cooked spinach with the Quark mixture and pour half into the flan tin. Make four indentations in the mixture and break an egg into each. Top with the rest of the mixture. Bake in an oven preheated to 200°C/400°F for 40-50 minutes until set. Serve hot or cold with lemon yoghurt.

Harzer Fondue

1 clove garlic, peeled and halved

2oz fat bacon or German speck, finely diced

1 cup milk

1lb Harzer cheese (or Emmentaler), grated

1oz butter

1 cup dry white wine

1 heaped tablespoon grated raw potato

1 tablespoon brandy

freshly ground black pepper

1 unsliced loaf of bread, for dipping

Rub the inside of a fondue pot with the cut sides of the garlic clove, then chop the garlic finely. Fry the garlic with the bacon in the fondue pot. Pour in the milk and add handfuls of cheese, stirring constantly until the cheese has melted. Add the butter and dry white wine and bring to a gentle boil. Stir in the grated potato and brandy, and bring back to the boil. Season with pepper and serve with large cubes of bread for dipping into the fondue.

Bavarian Cheese Balls

9oz German Camembert or Brie
2 tablespoons butter, softened
flour, for coating
1 egg, beaten
1 tablespoon fine breadcrumbs, for coating
butter, for frying
4 canned pear halves
4 cocktail cherries

Mash the cheese with a fork and mix well with the butter. With wet hands, divide the cheese into quarters and shape into 4 balls. Chill well. Roll each ball in flour, then beaten egg, and finally the breadcrumbs; make sure the balls are coated all over. Heat the butter in a skillet and fry the balls until golden brown all over. Arrange the pear halves on a plate, place a cheese ball on each and decorate with the cherries.

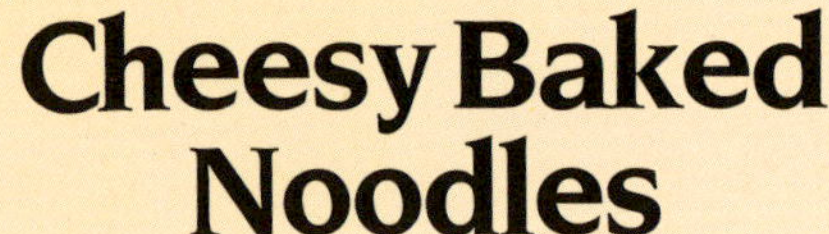

Cheesy Baked Noodles

½ lb dried ribbon noodles

salt & pepper

1 cup ham, cut into strips

2½oz butter

5 egg yolks

¾ cup grated Allgäu Emmentaler cheese

grated nutmeg, to taste

1 tablespoon butter

1 onion, peeled and finely chopped

2 tablespoons mixed herbs, finely chopped

2 tablespoons light cream

5 egg whites

2oz butter for greasing

Cook the noodles in boiling salted water for 10 minutes. Drain, refresh under cold water and leave to drain. Mix the ham with the noodles. Mix together the 2½oz butter, egg yolks and grated cheese, and season with salt, pepper and nutmeg. In a skillet, heat the butter and fry the onion until softened. Add the chopped herbs and cream. Add noodles and ham to the skillet and mix well until the noodles are well coated in sauce. Whisk the egg whites until stiff and place in bottom of buttered ovenproof dish. Spoon the noodles on top of the egg whites and bake in an oven preheated to 220°C/425°F for 30 minutes.

Tilsiter Puffs

1 packet instant white sauce mix (to make up to 1 pint)

1 tablespoon butter

6oz Tilsiter cheese, cubed

1 12oz packet frozen puff pastry, thawed

6 slices ham

1 egg, beaten

Prepare the white sauce according to the instructions on the packet. Add the butter and cubed cheese and stir well until cheese has melted. Roll out the puff pastry and cut with a sharp knife into 6 squares. Place a slice of ham in the middle of each and spread with the cheese sauce, keeping the edges of the pastry free from sauce. Brush the pastry edges with beaten egg, fold the pastry over to form triangles and press edges together well with a fork. Bake in an oven preheated to 200°C/400°F for 20-30 minutes until puffy and golden brown.

Eggs in Potato Nests

1½lbs potatoes, in their skins

salt

grated nutmeg

2 tablespoons butter

2 egg yolks

butter, for greasing

2½lbs fresh spinach, trimmed and washed

1 cup fat bacon or German speck, cut into cubes

8 eggs

paprika, to taste

lettuce leaves

2 tomatoes, quartered

Boil the potatoes until soft, then mash and combine with the salt, nutmeg, butter and egg yolks, beating until smooth. Spoon the mashed potato into a piping bag fitted with a large star nozzle and pipe into small nest shapes on a greased baking sheet. Blanch the spinach for 5 minutes in hot salted water, then drain and keep hot.

Fry the bacon in a skillet until crispy. Divide the spinach between the potato nests and scatter the bacon cubes over. Break an egg into each nest. Bake in an oven preheated to 180°C-200°C/350°F-400°F for 10-15 minutes until the eggs are set and the potato is lightly golden. Sprinkle the cooked eggs with salt and paprika.

To serve, arrange the nests on lettuce leaves and surround with tomato quarters.

Meat, Fish and Poultry

All German main meals are based on hearty portions of meat, poultry or fish. Beef, pork, chicken, goose, duck, trout and pike are well-established favorites.

Wine Grower's Rabbit

1 young rabbit, about 2lb, cut into small pieces

salt & pepper

3oz butter

2 onions, peeled and coarsely chopped

1 clove of garlic, peeled and chopped

1 teaspoon dried rosemary

1 teaspoon dried thyme

1 teaspoon dried sage

8 juniper berries, lightly crushed

about 1 cup dry red wine

1 teaspoon tomato purée

1 tablespoon heavy cream

Season the rabbit pieces with salt and pepper. Heat the butter in a large pan and add the onion, garlic, rosemary, thyme, sage and juniper berries. Add the rabbit pieces and cook until browned on all sides. Drain the fat from the pan, reduce the heat and add the red wine and tomato purée. Cover tightly and simmer over a medium heat for 40 minutes, if necessary adding a little more wine. Remove the rabbit to a warm serving dish and keep hot. Strain the cooking liquids into another pan and stir in the cream. Heat through gently then pour over the meat.

Wine Grower's Pigeons

6oz butter

1 teaspoon sugar

2 cups white wine (Riesling)

3 large cooking apples, peeled, cored and thinly sliced

2oz hazelnuts, coarsely chopped

2oz white raisins

1 teaspoon English mustard powder

4oz freshly made white breadcrumbs

4 small dressed pigeons

1lb black grapes, skinned (if liked) and halved

1 liqueur glass brandy

2 teaspoons hot mustard

salt & pepper

1 tablespoon heavy cream

apple slices, to garnish

To make the stuffing, melt 1 tablespoon of butter in a fireproof casserole, add the sugar and heat gently until it caramelizes and turns a golden brown. Add one glass of the wine, the apple slices, nuts and raisins and sprinkle the mustard powder over. Cook for about 2 minutes. Mix in the breadcrumbs. Use this mixture to stuff the pigeons then truss each one with string. Heat the remaining butter in a large fireproof casserole, add pigeons and cook until golden brown on all sides. Add the grapes and cook for a further 12 minutes. Remove the pigeons and grapes from the pan and keep warm. Add brandy and remaining wine to the juices in the pan and boil rapidly to reduce slightly. Add $\frac{1}{3}$ cup of water and the hot mustard, bring to the boil again and season with salt and pepper. Return the pigeons and grapes to the pan and heat through. Stir in the cream. To serve, arrange the pigeons on a platter, surrounded by the grapes, garnish with apple slices and serve the sauce separately.

Fillet Steak with Cherries

4 beef fillet steaks (5-6oz each)

2 tablespoons oil

2 cups cherries, washed and stoned

salt & pepper

½ glass red wine

1 tablespoon butter

Rub the oil into steaks. Fry the steaks in a very hot skillet for 4-8 minutes on both sides, then season with salt and pepper and keep warm. Add the wine, butter and cherries to the skillet and cook until cherries are soft. Pour the cherry sauce over the steaks and serve.

Roast Shoulder of Lamb

1 shoulder of lamb, unboned

salt

freshly ground black pepper

2oz butter, melted

Place the joint on rack in a roasting tin, sprinkle with salt and black pepper and pour the melted butter over. Roast in an oven preheated to 180°C/350°F for 20 minutes per pound, plus 20 minutes. Use the juice from the joint to make a gravy and serve with baby carrots, green beans and cauliflower florets.

Lamb's Liver on Apple Cubes

2oz butter

3 tablespoons sugar

1 glass German riesling wine

1 tablespoon cider vinegar

5 whole cloves

1 pinch ground cinnamon

$1\frac{1}{2}$lb apples, peeled, quartered and cut into cubes

$\frac{1}{2}$ teaspoon dried rosemary

8 slices lambs liver, about 2oz each

salt & pepper

Melt half the butter in a pan, add the sugar and heat gently until it caramelizes to a golden brown. Add the wine and the cider vinegar and stir over a low heat. Add the cloves, cinnamon, and apple cubes and cook until the apples are softened but still crunchy and most of the liquid has evaporated. Remove the cloves, and transfer to a heated serving dish. Melt the remaining butter in a skillet and add the rosemary. Fry the slices of liver carefully for about $1\frac{1}{2}$ minutes on each side, season with salt and pepper and serve on top of the apples.

Bockwurst Kebabs

Serves 2

4 German Bockwurst, cut into 1 inch pieces

1 onion, peeled and cut into wedges

½ cucumber, cut into 1 inch pieces then halved

1 red bell pepper, cored, seeded and cut into chunks

4oz piece fat bacon (or German speck) cut into chunks (optional)

melted butter, for brushing

Thread the ingredients alternately on to 4 kebab skewers. Brush with melted butter and cook under a preheated broiler for 15 minutes, turning frequently. Serve accompanied by curry sauce or a kebab sauce.

Salmon Steaks 'In The Bag'

½ cup chicken stock

3 carrots, peeled, cut into fine strips

4 small onions, peeled and halved

4 middle cut salmon steaks

white pepper

coarse sea salt

8oz mushrooms, sliced

2 teaspoons dried tarragon

2oz butter

1½ glasses dry German Sekt (sparkling white wine) or champagne

Heat the stock in a pan and boil the carrot strips and halved onions in it for about 10 minutes. Cut out four 12 inch square pieces of baking parchment, and place a quarter of the carrot strips on each. Top each with a raw salmon steak and season lightly with pepper and a few grains of sea salt. Place 2 onion halves, a quarter of the mushrooms, ½ teaspoon of tarragon and ½oz butter on each steak. Fold the paper over the steaks and close securely, then bake in an oven preheated to 165°C/325°F for 15-20 minutes. Serve the salmon steaks steaks in their wrappings, with boiled new potatoes.

Celebration Chicken with Mushrooms

3 tablespoons oil

½ cup lean belly bacon, cut into cubes

1 chicken, 3-4lb, jointed

1 cup silverskin onions

1 bell pepper, cored, seeded and sliced

2 tomatoes

juice of 1 lemon

freshly ground black pepper

salt

1-2 tablespoons flour

2 cups of good red wine

1½ cups fresh mushrooms, wiped and quartered

about ½ cup heavy cream

1 teaspoon of fresh parsley, finely chopped

Heat the oil in large pan and fry the bacon until crispy, then remove. Fry the chicken joints until browned then add the pearl onions, bell pepper, tomatoes, lemon juice and bacon. Sprinkle flour over and cook for a few minutes. Season with salt and black pepper. Stir in the wine and cook for 35 minutes. Remove the chicken joints and arrange them on a hot serving plate. Add the mushrooms to the sauce in the pan and add cream to taste. Pour the sauce over the chicken, sprinkle the chopped parsley over and serve.

Belly of Pork with Onion Sauce

4 slices of pork belly, about 1½lbs

salt & pepper

1 egg, beaten

4 tablespoons breadcrumbs

2oz fat

Sauce:

1oz fat

5oz onions, peeled and sliced

5oz apples, peeled and sliced

½ teaspoon dried thyme

1 cup water

1 packet instant gravy mix

Season the pork with salt and pepper and dip first into the beaten egg then into breadcrumbs to coat. Heat the fat in a skillet and fry the pork on each side for 6 minutes.

Meanwhile make the sauce. Heat the fat in a skillet and fry the onions and apples until golden brown. Sprinkle with the thyme. Add the water and stir in the gravy sauce mix to bind. If necessary season with more salt and pepper. Serve the pork accompanied by the sauce.

Ham with Cream

3 cups ham, cut into thin strips

¾ cup light cream

1 pot whole milk yoghurt

salt & pepper

sweet paprika

2 teaspoons tomato purée

1 cup grated cheese

1oz butter

Grease a fireproof dish with butter and lay the ham in it. Mix together the cream, yoghurt, salt, pepper, paprika and tomato purée and pour over the ham strips to cover. Sprinkle the grated cheese on and finally dot with the butter. Put the dish on the middle shelf of an oven preheated to 200°C/400°F and bake for about 10 minutes until the cheese has melted and browned.

Stuffed Marrow with Dill Cream Sauce

- 5oz Quark (low fat soft cheese)
- ½ pint soured cream
- freshly ground black pepper
- 3 bunches fresh dill, finely chopped
- 2 baby marrows or large zucchini, about 1lb each
- 2 onions, peeled and finely chopped
- 3oz butter
- 1lb ground beef
- salt
- thyme
- cayenne pepper, for sprinkling
- 4oz thinly sliced smoked ham

Whisk the Quark with the soured cream, season with salt and pepper and stir in the dill. Chill for two hours.

Peel the marrows or zucchini, halve them lengthwise and scoop out the seeds and flesh to leave boat-shaped shells. Heat 2 tablespoons of the butter in a large skillet and fry the onions until translucent. Add the ground beef and thyme, season with salt and brown for about 8 minutes. Place the marrow halves in a fireproof casserole and sprinkle with a little cayenne pepper. Line each one with slices of smoked ham then spoon the beef mixture on top. Bake in an oven preheated to 180°C/350°F for 25 minutes.

Serve the stuffed marrows hot, with cold dill cream sauce.

Saddle of Venison with Chestnut Butter

- saddle of venison
- salt & pepper
- 2 tablespoons butter
- ½ cup red wine
- 1 cup thickened meat stock (from a cube)
- ½ cup light cream
- cayenne pepper, to taste
- 3oz butter
- 8oz seedless grapes
- 6oz Pfefferlinge or chanterelles mushrooms
- 2oz bacon, diced
- 2 apples, peeled, halved and cored
- juice of 1 lemon
- 1 tablespoon apple juice
- 1 tablespoon sugar
- 4oz tinned chestnut purée (unsweetened)
- ¼ teaspoon ground cinnamon
- ¼ teaspoon ground cloves

Preheat the oven to 240°C/475°F. Rub the venison with salt and pepper. Melt the butter in a roasting tin, put the meat in the tin, place in the oven and reduce the heat to 200°C/400°F. Roast for 20 minutes per pound plus 20 minutes, basting frequently. Remove the venison to a warmed dish and pour off any surplus fat from the tin. Pour the wine into the roasting tin and bring to the boil, stirring well. Add the thickened meat stock, cream, cayenne pepper and lemon juice to taste. Carve the venison into ¼ to ½ inch thick slices, replace on the bone and keep warm.

For the sauce:

Melt 1oz of the butter in a skillet, add the grapes and chanterelles and fry gently for 5 minutes. Add the bacon and when crispy, spread the mixture over the saddle of venison. Put the apples in a pan, cover with water and add the lemon juice, apple juice and sugar. Bring to the boil then remove from the heat.

For the chestnut butter, cream the remaining 2oz of butter with the chestnut purée, cinnamon and ground cloves. Fill the warm apple halves with the chestnut butter and arrange them around the meat. Serve sauce separately.

Ham and Noodles

- 1 cup ham, cubed
- 2 tablespoons oil
- ½ head bok choy, sliced
- salt & pepper
- 1 cup water or meat stock (from a cube)
- ½lb dry egg noodles
- pinch of dried thyme

Heat the oil in a large pan and fry the ham lightly. Add the bok choy, season with salt and pepper and add the water or stock. Cover the pan and cook for 20 minutes. Meanwhile cook the noodles in boiling salted water and drain. Add the noodles to the ham mixture, season with pepper and a pinch of thyme, and serve.

Wurst Kebab

- 1lb firm German sausage (such as Schinkenwurst or Bierwurst), cut into cubes
- 1 medium salad gherkin, cut into cubes
- 4oz sliced Canadian bacon
- 8 cherry tomatoes
- salt
- coarsely ground black pepper
- oil, for coating

Thread the sausage, gherkin, rolled bacon slices and tomatoes on to kebab skewers, brush with oil and season with salt and pepper. Broil for 4 minutes on both sides.

Brisket of Beef with Herb Sauce

- 1 joint (pickled) beef brisket, weighing about 2lbs
- 4 cups water
- 1 onion, left whole
- 1 bayleaf, fresh
- 2 cups hot white sauce
- 1 bouquet garni
- 1 bunch dill, chopped; 1 bunch parsley, chopped; 1 bunch chives, chopped — to taste
- 2 tablespoons cream
- pepper
- celery salt

Simmer the beef in the water (without salt) with the onion and bayleaf for about 1½ hours. Meanwhile, make the sauce. Bring the white sauce to the boil. Cook the bouquet garni briefly in the sauce then remove and add the chopped herbs. Thin the sauce with the cream and add pepper and celery salt to taste. Serve the meat together with the herb sauce.

Boiled Beef with Onion Sauce

- 3lbs beef, silverside
- 1oz butter
- 6 small onions, peeled and sliced
- 1oz flour
- 2 tablespoons wine vinegar
- 1 pint beef stock (from a cube)
- 1 tablespoon tomato purée
- 2 garlic cloves, peeled and crushed
- salt
- freshly ground black pepper

Boil or pot roast beef until cooked. Heat the butter and fry the onions for about 5 minutes until browned. Add the flour and continue to cook for 1 minute. Slowly add the wine vinegar and beef stock, stirring continuously. Add the tomato purée and garlic, and season with salt and black pepper. Simmer for 20 minutes. Slice the cooked beef, and serve with sliced glazed carrots accompanied by the sauce.

Beer Roast

- 3lb roasting joint of beef
- salt & pepper
- 2 tablespoons beef dripping
- 1½ pints German beer
- 1 leek, washed and sliced
- 2 green bell peppers, seeded and sliced
- 2 carrots, sliced
- ¼ head of celery, sliced
- 2 cups onions, peeled and chopped
- 4 cups button mushrooms, left whole
- 1 teaspoon flour
- ½ cup light cream

Season the meat well with salt and pepper, rubbing the seasonings in well. Heat the dripping in a roasting tin and brown the meat all over in an oven preheated to 180°C/350°F. Pour over two thirds of the beer and cook for 30 minutes. Then add the leek, peppers, carrots, celery, onion and mushrooms and cook for 1 hour more. Transfer the beef to a heated serving platter. Add the remaining beer to the sauces in the pan, stir in the flour, then pour in the cream. Stir until thickened over a gentle heat. Serve the meat with the sauce and with parsley potatoes.

Steak Salad with Croûtons

11 oz cornsalad

1 medium onion, peeled and finely chopped

6 tablespoons red wine vinegar

$\frac{1}{2}$ teaspoon sugar

2 tablespoons oil

salt & white pepper

8oz lean steak, cut into strips

2oz butter

4oz stale white bread, cut into cubes

Place the cornsalad in a bowl and sprinkle the finely chopped onion over. Mix the red wine vinegar with sugar and oil, pour over the salad, and season with salt and pepper. Season the steak with salt and pepper, heat half the butter in a skillet and fry quickly until browned but pink inside. Remove and add to the salad. Heat the remaining butter in the same skillet and fry the bread until crisp, then add to the salad. Toss the salad and serve as a complete meal.

Sauerbraten

6 tablespoons red wine

6 tablespoons red wine vinegar

1 cup water

2 bay leaves

6 peppercorns

4 juniper berries, lightly crushed

joint lean rolled beef, about 3lb

1 large onion, peeled and sliced

1 oz butter

2 large carrots, peeled and sliced

salt & pepper

1 oz flour

$\frac{1}{2}$ cup soured cream

Put the first six ingredients in a pan and bring to the boil. Cool. Place beef in a large bowl with the onion, pour in the wine mixture, cover and leave to marinate for 2-3 days in a cool place, turning meat several times. Remove and pat dry. Melt the butter in a pan and brown the meat all over. Transfer the joint to a fireproof casserole. Take the onions from the marinade, drain and brown in the same fat with the carrots. Add the marinade, bring to boil then pour over beef. Cover and either simmer on top of the stove (depending on the cut), or bake in an oven preheated to 180°C/350°F for $1\frac{1}{2}$-4 hours until tender. Remove the joint and the vegetables and keep hot. Skim the fat from the liquid in the casserole. Blend the flour with soured cream and a little of the liquid until smooth, then whisk back into the rest of the liquid. Simmer for 2 minutes, stirring, then taste and adjust the seasonings. Spoon a little sauce over meat to moisten and serve rest separately.

Bacon and Plums

1 lb smoked belly bacon, cut into slices
1 large onion, peeled and chopped
2½ lbs plums, halved and pitted
juice of ½ lemon
1 tablespoon sugar
2 tablespoons white wine
½ cup water

Fry bacon lightly in a skillet. Add the onion and fry until translucent. Layer the bacon and onion with the plums in a buttered fireproof dish. Mix lemon juice, sugar, wine and water and pour over plums. Bake in an oven preheated to 200°C/400°F for 50-60 minutes.

Lamb and Potato Stew

3lb stewing lamb, cut into cubes
3 carrots, peeled andsliced
3 leeks, washed and sliced
salt & pepper
1 bouquet garni
$1\frac{1}{2}$ pints meat stock (from a cube)
12 small potatoes, peeled
12 small pickling onions, peeled
2 sticks celery, chopped
1 oz butter, cut into pieces

Layer the lamb, carrots and leeks in a fireproof casserole, seasoning each layer with salt and pepper, and putting the bouquet garni in between the middle layers. Add enough meat stock to cover the stew and cook in an oven pre-heated to 200°C/400°F for about $1\frac{1}{2}$ hours. Add the potatoes, pickling onions and celery and top with pieces of butter. Cover the casserole and cook for a further 45 minutes.

German Lamb Stew

serves 6

$1\frac{1}{2}$ pints meat stock (from a cube)
2lbs neck or breast of lamb, diced
1 large onion, peeled and diced
1 leek, washed and diced
1 medium celery head, diced
9oz potatoes, peeled and chopped
1 medium cauliflower, broken into florets
salt
freshly ground black pepper
1 tablespoon fresh parsley, chopped

Put the meat stock in a large pan and stew the lamb, onion, leek and celery for about 45 minutes. Add the potatoes and cauliflower and season to taste with salt and pepper, cooking until the meat and vegetables are tender, about 30-40 minutes. Serve sprinkled with chopped fresh parsley.

Leg of Beef in Vodka

- 4oz smoked fat bacon, cut into thick strips
- 1 small glass of vodka
- leg of beef joint, weighing about 6lb
- salt & pepper
- 2 tablespoons dripping
- 2 onions, peeled and cut into rings
- 2 cups hot meat stock
- 1 tablespoon flour
- 2 cups soured cream
- 1½ tablespoons German mustard
- 1 dash of red wine
- 2 slices beet, cut into strips
- 1 salad gherkin, cut into strips
- 1 bunch of dill, chopped

Sprinkle the vodka over the bacon. Cover and refrigerate for 30 minutes. Press the bacon strips onto the beef and rub all over with pepper and salt. Melt the dripping in a roasting tin, add the leg of beef and the onions and roast for 30 minutes in an oven preheated to 180°C/350°F. Pour on the hot meat stock and return to oven, covered, for 2 hours. Transfer the beef to a heated platter and stir the flour into the meat juices in the tin. Allow to cook for a further 5 minutes. Mix in the soured cream, mustard, red wine, beet and gherkin. Add half of the chopped dill and cook for 5 minutes. Cut the meat into slices and serve with the sauce, garnished with the remaining dill. Serve with boiled potatoes and a salad.

Veal Escalopes with Mussels

- 20 cooked mussels, shelled
- 4 veal escalopes, 4-5oz each
- salt
- 2oz butter, for frying
- 1 glass German white wine
- 4 tablespoons light cream
- 2 tablespoons butter
- sprigs of fresh fennel or dill, to garnish

Melt the 1oz of the butter in a skillet and fry the mussels. Remove and keep warm. Heat the remaining butter in another skillet and fry the escalopes over a high heat, seasoning with a little salt until golden and cooked. Remove from the heat and keep warm with the mussels. Combine the cooking juices from the mussels and the veal in one skillet and add white wine. Boil for about 2 minutes, stirring, then add the cream and remaining butter and mix well. Lay escalopes and mussels on a serving dish and pour the sauce over. Garnish with fennel or fresh dill.

Veal Stuffed Spring Cabbage

1 lb veal, cut into small dice

salt & pepper

2oz butter

1 onion, peeled and chopped

1 clove garlic, peeled and chopped

6oz mushrooms, wiped and finely chopped

1 tablespoon heavy cream

1 tablespoon fresh mixed herbs, chopped

12-16 spring cabbage leaves

grated nutmeg

½ cup white wine

extra heavy cream

Season the veal with salt and pepper. Heat the 2oz of butter in a skillet and slowly fry the veal with the onion and garlic until the onion is translucent. Add the mushrooms and cook for a further 5 minutes. Remove from the heat, fold in the cream and the herbs. Boil the cabbage leaves for 1-2 minutes in salted water until slightly softened, then drain thoroughly and lay out flat on a board. Cut away the hard stalks. Place two tablespoons of the veal mixture on each leaf, fold in the sides and roll the leaf up into a parcel. Butter a fireproof covered dish, place the parcels in it, place a knob of butter on each parcel and grate over a little nutmeg. Pour over the wine, cover with tightly fitting lid and cook for about 25 minutes in an oven preheated to 220°C/425°F. Remove the parcels to a heated serving platter, thicken the juices in the dish with a little heavy cream and pour the sauce over the parcels.

German Style School Sandwich

1 slice of Volkornbrot

butter, for spreading

2 carrots, grated

½ apple, thinly sliced

1 cup cooked chicken, minced

Spread the bread with butter. Arrange the carrots and apple on the bread and lay the chicken on top.

Duck with Apple

2 tablespoons lard

1 duck, washed and cleaned, weighing about 5lb

3 tablespoons redcurrant jelly

2 dessert apples, sliced

4 cloves

salt & pepper

Heat the lard in a roasting tin in the oven and brown the duck in it on all sides. Continue cooking in an oven preheated to 180°C/350°F for 1½ hours, basting frequently with the duck's juices. Remove to a heated serving platter. Melt the redcurrant jelly in the meat juices left in the pan over a low heat. Add the apple slices and cloves and cook for about 4 minutes. Season with salt and pepper. Remove cloves and serve the duck, accompanied by the sauce.

Primadonna Steaks

serves 2

2oz butter

pinch of garlic powder

pinch of salt

2 teaspoons fresh chopped herbs

¼ teaspoon salt

¼ teaspoon celery salt

pinch of dried sage

½ teaspoon cayenne

3-4 tablespoons oil

2 beef steaks, about 5-6oz each

2 slices fresh truffle

Mix the butter with garlic powder, salt and herbs and shape it into a small sausage. Chill. Combine the salt, celery salt, sage and cayenne pepper, rub the steaks with this mixture. Brush both sides of each steak very liberally with oil and leave them, one on top of the other, for at least 30 minutes. Without adding any additional fat, fry the steaks on both sides in a hot skillet until cooked to your liking. Cut the chilled herb butter into slices and lay them on the cooked steaks. Serve with the slices of truffle.

Stuffed Veal Heart

- 1 veal heart
- 4oz white bread
- 1 cup milk
- 8oz ground pork or beef
- salt & pepper
- pinch of nutmeg
- $\frac{1}{2}$ teaspoon paprika
- 2oz dried brown mushrooms (Pfefferlinge), stems removed and soaked in cold water for 1 hour
- 3 tablespoons butter
- 1 onion, peeled and finely chopped
- 8oz celery, diced
- 10 small pickling onions, peeled
- 1 glass red wine
- 1 bouquet garni

Cut open the heart. Soak the bread in the milk, squeeze out the surplus milk and mix the bread with the ground pork or beef. Season with salt and pepper and add the nutmeg and paprika. Squeeze out the dried mushrooms. Heat 2 tablespoons of the butter in a skillet and lightly fry the mushrooms with the onion and celery. Cool and mix well with the meat mixture. Use to stuff the heart and tie securely with string. Heat the remaining butter in a heavy-based fireproof casserole and brown the heart all over. Add the pickling onions, red wine and the bouquet garni. Cover and bake in an oven preheated to 165°C/325°F, for $2\frac{1}{2}$ hours, adding a little hot water to the casserole from time to time. When ready to eat, cut the heart into quarters, remove the bouquet garni and serve.

Fillet of Lamb with Fruit

serves 2

- 2 lamb fillets (cut into $\frac{3}{4}$ inch strips)
- flour, for coating
- salt
- freshly ground black pepper
- 2oz butter

To serve:

- pineapple, pear or apple pieces
- hot creamed potatoes

Dip the strips of lamb into flour to coat then season with salt and pepper. Heat the butter in a skillet and fry the meat quickly until it is browned but juicy. Remove from skillet and keep warm. Fry the fruit in the remaining fat in the skillet until heated through. Pipe the outline of a large heart shape with the creamed potatoes on a warm plate and place the fruit and lamb in the middle. Serve with a German Riesling wine.

Veal Casserole

$1\frac{1}{2}$lbs breast of veal, cut into cubes

2 cups water

$\frac{1}{2}$ head bok choy, sliced

4 medium potatoes, peeled and sliced

1 cup green beans, cut to 1 inch lengths

1 red bell pepper, cubed

4 tomatoes, sliced

1 leek, washed and sliced

$\frac{1}{4}$ head of celery, sliced

salt & pepper

sugar, to taste

chopped fresh parsley, to garnish

Put the veal and water into a large pan, bring to boil and simmer for 30 minutes. Layer the vegetables on top of the meat, season with salt, pepper and sugar, and cook for a further 30 minutes over a medium heat. Sprinkle with parsley to serve.

Veal Medallions on Spinach and Tomato Bases

- 9oz spinach, washed and trimmed
- salt & pepper
- 2 large tomatoes, peeled, seeded and cut into dice
- 3oz butter
- 8 fresh sage leaves
- 4 veal medallions, about 6oz each
- sage leaves, to garnish

Cook the spinach for 2 minutes in salted water. Butter four small tartlet tins and line with the spinach leaves. Heat 1oz of the butter in a pan and stew the tomatoes for 6 minutes. Spread the tomato mixture over the spinach, season with salt and pepper and bake in an oven preheated to 180°C/350°F for about 15 minutes. Season medallions with salt and pepper. Melt the remaining 2oz butter in a skillet (do not allow to brown), add sage leaves and fry the meat for about 10-12 minutes until golden brown. Remove tomato-spinach cases from tins and top each one with a veal medallion, garnish with sage leaves.

Top Rib Steak

serves 2

$1\frac{1}{2}$lbs top rib steak
salt & pepper
cayenne pepper
1 tablespoon fresh basil, chopped
1 cup clear meat stock
1 tablespoon dripping
1 15oz can peeled tomatoes

Season the steak well with pepper, salt, cayenne and basil and leave to stand for 30 minutes. Heat a skillet and fry the steak on both sides without fat. When it is browned add the meat stock, cover and cook for up to 1 hour.

Thoroughly grease a fireproof dish with the dripping and pour in the tomatoes with their juice. Lay the steak on top and cook on the center shelf of an oven preheated to 180°C/350°F for 20 minutes until the steak is tender.

Chicken Fricassée

1 chicken, weighing about 3-4lb
1 pint chicken stock, cube or fresh
2 onions, peeled and finely chopped
2 tablespoons butter
2 tablespoons flour
2 glasses white wine
salt & pepper
1 tablespoon lemon juice
2 tablespoons heavy cream
1 egg yolk
8oz cooked veal, cut into cubes
7oz can asparagus, drained
7oz can mushrooms, drained

Simmer the chicken in the stock in a large covered pan for 1 hour, then remove the skin and bones and cut the meat into large pieces, reserving the stock. Sauté the onions in butter until translucent, sprinkle with flour and leave for a few minutes or so. Pour on $2\frac{1}{2}$ cups of the chicken stock and stir in the wine, salt, pepper and lemon juice and cook until thickened. Whip cream and egg yolk and stir in. Add the veal, asparagus and mushrooms to the sauce and heat through.

Trout with Basil and Tomatoes

- 4 small trout, cleaned and washed
- juice of 1 lemon
- salt, to taste
- 1 bunch fresh basil, stalks removed
- 1 stick butter
- 4 medium-sized tomatoes, peeled, seeded and cut into dice
- freshly ground black pepper

Rub the insides of the trout with lemon juice and salt and insert a few of the basil leaves into the body cavity of each. Melt the butter in a skillet, add the remaining basil leaves and then the trout. Fry over a low heat for about 20 minutes until cooked, adding the tomatoes and a grinding of pepper after about 15 minutes. Serve the trout on a bed of the tomato and basil mixture, with any cooking juices poured over.

Chicken on a Bed of Vegetables

- 1 chicken, weighing about 3-4lb
- salt & pepper
- 2 teaspoons fresh thyme
- 3oz butter
- fresh vegetables according to season: e.g. kohlrabi, leeks, celery, red cabbage, carrots, washed and cut into small pieces
- $\frac{3}{4}$ pint chicken stock, cube or fresh

Season the chicken with salt and pepper and rub with the thyme. Melt the butter in a casserole and cook the chicken until crisp on all sides. Remove the chicken and keep warm. Add the chosen vegetables to the pan and cook briefly in the butter. Lay the chicken on top of the vegetables and add the stock. Cover and cook for about 40 minutes.

Chicken in White Wine

- 2 capons, about 6-7lb each
- 2oz butter
- $1\frac{1}{2}$ cups onions, peeled and chopped
- 5 shallots, peeled and chopped
- 1 bundle fresh tarragon
- 1 sprig fresh thyme
- 1 sprig fresh parsley, chopped
- 2 tablespoons flour
- 3 cups white wine
- $\frac{1}{2}$ cup heavy cream
- salt & pepper

Divide each capon into 4 and season each piece with salt and pepper. Melt the butter in a large pan, add the capons and cook briefly until browned on all sides. Add the onions, shallots, tarragon, thyme, half the parsley and the flour. Pour in the white wine and cook slowly for about 45 minutes. Stir in the cream and season with salt and pepper to taste. Sprinkle the remaining parsley over before serving.

Chicken with Tomatoes

- 2 chickens, about 3lb each
- salt & pepper
- 1 cup oil
- 4-6 tomatoes, peeled
- 3 garlic cloves, peeled and crushed
- 1 bay leaf
- 1-2 cloves
- 3-4oz can tomato purée
- 1 teaspoon sugar
- 2 cups dry white wine
- 1 teaspoon dried thyme
- 3 tablespoons brandy

Season the chickens inside and out with salt and pepper. Heat the oil in a very large pan and gently fry the chickens until brown on all sides. Cover the pan and leave the chickens to cook over a low heat for about 1½ hours. Add the tomatoes to the pan and add the garlic, bay leaf, cloves, tomato purée, sugar and white wine. Cook for about 15 minutes. Stir and add thyme and brandy to taste. Remove the cooked chickens and cut each one into four portions. Put in a large dish and pour the sauce over.

Gourmet's Chicken

1 chicken, weighing about $2\frac{1}{2}$lbs, washed and dried

5oz rashers fat bacon or German speck slices

salt

1oz butter, melted

parsley sprigs, to garnish

Sauce:

1oz butter

1 tablespoon flour

$\frac{1}{2}$ cup German white wine

1 cup meat stock (from a cube)

$\frac{1}{2}$ cup heavy cream

salt & white pepper

pinch sugar

few drops of lemon juice

2 egg yolks

15oz tin round carrots, drained

1 cup sliced mushrooms

Cover thighs of the chicken with the bacon or speck slices. Rub the rest of the chicken skin with salt and brush with the melted butter. Roast in an oven preheated to 200°C/400°F for $1\frac{1}{4}$ hours.

To make the sauce, heat the butter in a pan, stir in the flour, cook, stirring, for 1 minute then add in the wine, stock and cream. Cook, stirring continuously, until thickened, then season with salt and pepper, sugar and lemon juice and beat in the egg yolks. Add the mushrooms and carrots and bring to the boil. When ready to serve, place the chicken on a serving platter, pour the sauce over, arrange vegetables around it and garnish with parsley.

Gourmet Sausage Toast

4 slices rye bread

1oz lard

4 slices white bread

1oz butter

2 eggs, beaten

$\frac{1}{2}$ tablespoon fresh chives, finely chopped

$\frac{1}{2}$ tablespoon fresh parsley, finely chopped

2 large tomatoes, sliced

4 slices of 2 different types of firm German sausage

2 radishes, grated

oil, for brushing

lettuce, to serve

parsley, to garnish

Lightly toast the rye bread under the broiler and spread with lard. Butter the white bread. Heat more butter in a small pan, add the eggs, parsley and chives and cook over a gentle heat, stirring continuously, until the eggs are scrambled. Brush the slices of sausage with oil and broil until they curl. Fill half the sausage curls with grated radish and the remainder with scrambled egg. Lay tomato slices on all the slices of bread and arrange stuffed sausage slices on top. Serve on lettuce leaves, garnishing with parsley.

German Blutwurst (Blackpudding) with Apples

2oz butter

2 sharp-tasting dessert apples, cored and cut into thick slices

pinch of salt

pinch of cinnamon

1 German blutwurst (blackpudding) ring

Melt the butter in a skillet, add the apple slices and cook until lightly browned. Sprinkle with salt and cinnamon. Prick the skin of the blutwurst, add to the pan and fry gently until crisp on the outside, about 5 minutes. Serve the blutwurst straight from the skillet, cut into slices, with the apples.

Roast Turkey Roll

1 rolled turkey roasting joint, weighing about 2-3lb

salt & pepper

3 tablespoons oil

4oz bacon slices

Season the turkey roll with salt and pepper. Heat the oil in a roasting pan and brown the roll quickly on all sides. Lay the bacon rashers on top so that the joint remains juicy during cooking and roast for about 60 minutes in the oven preheated to 200°C/400°F.

Turkey Steaks with Cheese

4 turkey steaks, about 5-6oz each

salt & pepper

2-3 tablespoons grated Allgäu Emmentaler cheese

6 tablespoons breadcrumbs

2 eggs, beaten

oil, for frying

Season the turkey steaks with salt and pepper. Mix the cheese with the breadcrumbs. Dip the steaks in beaten egg and then dip them in the mixed cheese and bread-crumbs. Heat the oil in the pan and fry the turkey steaks on both sides until browned. Serve immediately.

Country Braised Chicken Legs

4 chicken legs

salt & pepper

2oz butter

1 teaspoon dried rosemary

4 tomatoes, peeled and chopped

4 onions, peeled

cloves

4oz breakfast bacon

3 tablespoons catsup

1 tablespoon soy sauce

Season the chicken legs with salt and pepper. Melt the butter in a pan and fry the legs with the rosemary until golden. Remove from the pan. Press the cloves into the onions then add the bacon, tomatoes and onions to the pan and cook gently. Stir in the catsup and soy sauce, return the legs to the pan and cook for a good 15 minutes, until tender and cooked through.

Mustard Butter Sauce

2 sticks butter
2 egg yolks
5oz sharp mustard or horseradish mustard
1 cup light cream
1 cup natural yoghurt

Melt the butter in a heavy-based pan. Whisk the egg yolks and mustard together in a flameproof casserole then place over a gentle heat to warm through, then remove the pan from the heat. Off the heat, slowly pour the melted butter in to the egg yolk mixture, whisking all the time. Mix together cream and yoghurt and stir into the mixture. Heat through gently. (Do not boil.) If the sauce is too thick add one tablespoon water to thin down slightly. This sauce is good with fish or poached eggs.

Steak and Bacon

serves 2

- 2 tablespoons butter, for frying
- 2 rib steaks, 6-7oz each
- salt
- freshly ground black pepper
- 4 rashers bacon
- 1 stick butter
- 2 tablespoons fresh chives, chopped
- 1 teaspoon onion, finely chopped
- 2 tablespoons white wine vinegar
- 1 tablespoon cold water
- 2 egg yolks
- juice of $\frac{1}{2}$ a lemon
- tomato wedges, to decorate
- 2 slices fried bread, to serve

Heat butter in a large skillet and fry the steaks until done to your liking. Season to taste with salt and black pepper, and keep warm. Fry the bacon slices in the same way and keep warm.

Melt the remaining butter in a pan over a low heat and allow to cool slightly. Combine 1 teaspoon of the chives, the chopped onion and the wine vinegar in a separate saucepan and season with pepper. Boil until the vinegar has reduced to a scant tablespoon. Remove from the heat and add the cold water, then stir in the egg yolks. Whisk over a low heat until thick and frothy. Remove from the heat again and slowly whisk in the melted butter. Whisk in the lemon juice, and season with salt.

To serve, arrange the steaks and bacon on the fried bread and pour the sauce over. Garnish with the remaining chives and wedges of tomato.

Cold Meat Platter

Choose as wide a variety of cold meats as you can and arrange them attractively on platters. From the front, those in the picture are: sliced Zungenwurst (tongue sausage), rolls of German Salami, sliced fine Cervelat, rolled Westphalian ham, sliced German Salami (with garlic) cornets or Bierwurst.

Sweet and Sauerkraut

- $1\frac{1}{2}$oz butter
- 2 onions, peeled and finely chopped
- 1 lb can sauerkraut, drained
- generous cup unsweetened pineapple juice
- 1 small ripe pineapple (or 1 lb can pineapple cubes)
- salt & pepper
- pinch of sugar

Heat the butter in a pan and fry the onions until soft. Add the sauerkraut and pineapple juice. Bring to the boil, stirring with a fork. Cover and simmer for 10 minutes. Cut the top off the pineapple and scoop out flesh, discarding the tough central core. Dice the flesh and add to the pan, then stir well. If using canned pineapple cubes drain, season well and add to the pan. Spoon the mixture into the shell of the pineapple or a bowl, adding a little boiled sauerkraut dressing if desired. Chill thoroughly. Serve as a salad, or as an accompaniment to a platter of hot German sausages.

Hot Doggery

Prepare a selection of hot Frankfurters, wieners, bockwurst and bratwurst (see below), on a warm plate and keep hot. Serve with Mustard Dip or Tomato Dip (see below) for dunking to add extra zip.

The correct way to warm up Frankfurters and wieners is to bring a large pan of water to the boil, remove from the heat and add the sausages. Return to a very low heat (the water should barely simmer) for 5-6 minutes, then drain. The sausages should never, ever, fast boil. Bockwurst and bratwurst should be grilled or fried, but for exact times etc., follow the instructions on the packets, as individual types can vary.

Mustard Dip

2 teaspoons German mustard

½ cup natural yoghurt

1 tablespoon onion, finely chopped

1 pickled gherkin, finely chopped

grated rind of ½ a lemon

freshly chopped parsley, to garnish

salt

freshly ground black pepper

Combine all the ingredients and season to taste with salt and freshly ground black pepper.

Tomato Dip

6 tablespoons egg mayonnaise

2 tablespoons tomato catsup

1 teaspoon Worcestershire Sauce

1 teaspoon lemon juice

2 tomatoes, peeled and chopped

1 tablespoon finely chopped onion

1 tablespoon chopped capers

salt

freshly ground black pepper

Combine all the ingredients and season to taste with salt and freshly ground black pepper.

This page: above, **Sweet and Sauerkraut,** *below,* **Cold Meat Platter.**

Potatoes and Dumplings

Potatoes and potato dumplings are particularly popular in the North of Germany while noodles are more commonly served in the South.

Potatoes with Cheesy Tomato Sauce

1lb potatoes
salt
2 onions, peeled and chopped
1 tablespoon butter
3 large tomatoes
$\frac{1}{2}$ teaspoon freshly ground black pepper
$\frac{1}{2}$ teaspoon cayenne pepper
$\frac{1}{8}$ teaspoon caraway seeds
$\frac{1}{4}$ cup milk
5oz Allgäu Emmentaler cheese, grated
butter, for greasing

Boil the potatoes in salted water until soft then peel, halve and keep warm. Heat the butter in a skillet and fry the onions until golden brown. Plunge the tomatoes into boiling water for several seconds then remove, slip off the skins and cut into small pieces. Add the tomatoes to the onions and cook for 5 minutes. Add the pepper, cayenne pepper, salt, caraway seeds and milk. Mix in the grated cheese and stir until melted. Do not let it cook. Grease a flat gratin dish with butter. Arrange the potatoes in the dish, the cut side uppermost. Pour the hot thick tomato-cheese sauce over the potatoes and serve immediately.

Creamy Baked Potatoes

2lb potatoes, peeled and thinly sliced

2oz butter

½ cup light cream

½ cup milk

2oz grated cheese

1 tablespoon fresh parsley, chopped

Butter a 2 pint soufflé dish and layer potatoes inside (do not use all the butter). Cover potatoes with the cream, milk, salt and pepper. Sprinkle with grated cheese, knobs of remaining butter, and parsley. Bake at 220°C/425°F for about 30 minutes.

Potato, Chicken and Bean Salad

several fresh salad leaves

4 large tomatoes, sliced

3 large potatoes, cooked, peeled and sliced

2 cups cooked green beans

2 cups cooked chicken, cubed

1 cup olives, stoned

2 hard-boiled eggs, quartered

1 cup vinaigrette dressing

3 tablespoons fresh parsley, chopped

8-10 anchovy fillets

Lay the salad leaves in a shallow dish and arrange a layer of tomato and potato slices on top. Arrange the beans and chicken meat on top of these and decorate with the olives and with quartered hard-boiled eggs. Then sprinkle the vinaigrette dressing and chopped parsley over and finally place the anchovy fillets on top. Serve with crusty bread.

Potatoes with Leeks

2lbs potatoes, peeled

salt

2 tablespoons butter

1 tablespoon milk

1lb leeks, sliced

1 red bell pepper, cored, seeded and sliced

2 cups hot chicken stock

Boil the potatoes in salted water until soft. Drain and then mash, adding the butter and milk. Keep warm. Cook the leeks and bell pepper in the stock until soft. Drain and mix into the mashed potato. Serve with green salad or roast ham.

Dainty Potato Rolls

- 2lbs potatoes, peeled
- 2 cups flour
- 2lbs ground beef
- 1 onion, peeled and chopped
- 2 tablespoons fresh breadcrumbs
- 1 egg
- 2 tablespoons fresh parsley, chopped
- salt & pepper
- 3-4 tablespoons oil or butter

Boil the potatoes for 20 minutes in salted water until tender then mash and mix with the flour. Meanwhile mix the ground beef with the chopped onion, breadcrumbs, egg, parsley, salt and pepper. Knead the potato mixture well and roll it out to about ½ inch thickness on a floured board. Spread the beef over the dough and roll it up. Heat the oil or butter in a skillet, cut ½ inch slices from the roll and fry on both sides until golden brown.

Baked Potato Fans

- 2lbs medium-sized potatoes, peeled
- salt
- freshly ground black pepper or caraway seeds
- 2 tablespoons butter, cut into pieces
- ½-1 cup grated Allgäu Emmentaler cheese

Lay the potatoes flat and slice thinly at regular intervals, not cutting through to the bottom of the potatoes. Season with salt and pepper or caraway seeds. Place the potatoes in a buttered fireproof dish and dot with butter pieces. Bake for about 30 minutes in an oven preheated to 200°C/400°F until crisp and cooked through. Sprinkle with grated cheese and return to oven for 5-10 minutes until the cheese has melted. Serve immediately.

Potato and Egg Salad

½lb firm potatoes

½ cup meat stock

salt & pepper

4 tablespoons oil

1 tablespoon butter

2 cups cleaned and thinly sliced mushrooms

lettuce leaves

1 hard-boiled egg, peeled and chopped

1 shallot, peeled and finely chopped

2 tablespoons vinegar

1 tablespoon German mustard

Wash the potatoes and cook them in their skins. Allow to cool, then peel and slice. Combine the meat stock, salt, pepper and 1 tablespoon of the oil and put the potatoes in this to marinate. Heat the butter in a skillet and fry the mushrooms. Mix them with the lettuce leaves and put in a salad bowl. Lay the potatoes on top. Combine the hard-boiled egg, shallot, vinegar, mustard and remaining oil and pour this over the salad. Mix well, then leave before serving to allow the flavors to penetrate.

Farmer's Quark Breakfast

3 onions, peeled and chopped

7oz smoked bacon, finely diced

1lb boiled potatoes, thickly sliced

5 eggs

1 cup Quark (low fat soft cheese)

1 tablespoon soured cream or yoghurt

1 teaspoon caraway seeds

Fry the onions and bacon in a large skillet until transparent and slightly browned. Add the potatoes and fry until golden brown. Whisk together the eggs, Quark, cream or yoghurt and caraway seeds, pour over the potatoes and let the mixture cook over a low heat until it has set into the consistency of an omelette. Serve immediately, straight from the skillet.

Sauerkraut Dumplings

1 cup sauerkraut

½ onion, peeled and finely chopped

salt & pepper

2 cups hot water

1 packet potato dumpling mix

Mix all ingredients together and shape into 8-10 dumplings. Boil for 10-15 minutes until cooked through.

Bacon and Potato Kebabs

4 large baking potatoes, washed and cut into slices

salt

freshly ground black pepper

2lb large onions, peeled

1 teaspoon caraway seeds

½ cup sliced lean smoked bacon

cayenne pepper, to taste

1-2 tablespoons butter

Dry the potato sticks on kitchen paper and place side by side on the work surface. Sprinkle with a little salt and pepper and rub in. Cut the onions into ¼ inch thick slices, placing them side by side. Sprinkle the caraway seeds over one side and rub in. Rub the cayenne pepper into one side of the bacon.

Leave the seasoned potatoes, onions and bacon to stand for 10 minutes, then thread them alternately on to skewers, impaling the end sticks of the potatoes at the beginning and end of the skewer. Brush with butter, cover with foil and place in preheated oven at maximum heat. Cook for 30 minutes and then serve in the foil wrappings.

Cheese Fries

2lbs potatoes, peeled and cut into matchstick strips

oil, for frying

1 cup grated Allgäu Emmentaler cheese

cress, to garnish

1 tablespoon fresh chives, chopped

½lb tomatoes, sliced

Heat the oil in a frying pan and deep fry the potatoes until golden brown. Drain, and place in a fire-proof dish. Sprinkle the grated cheese over and place under a pre-heated broiler to brown. Serve garnished with cress and chives and accompanied by tomato slices.

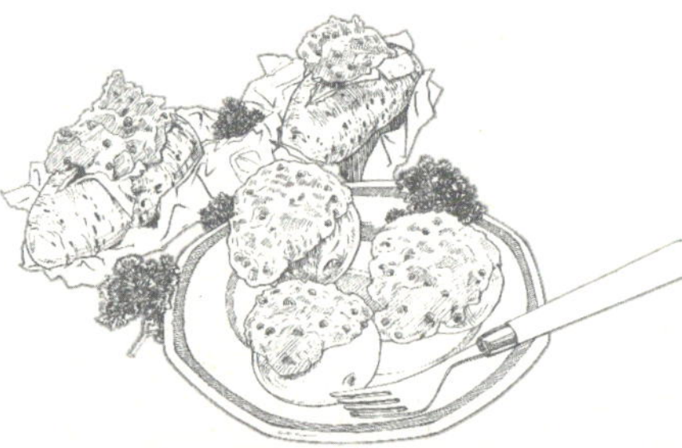

Potato Bake

1lb firm potatoes, peeled and coarsely grated

2 onions, peeled and coarsely grated

2 teaspoons fresh parsley, finely chopped

1 teaspoon celery seeds

2 tablespoons butter, plus extra for baking

¼ teaspoon pepper

1 teaspoon salt

Preheat the oven to 200°C/400°F. Thoroughly mix all ingredients in a large bowl. Grease a 2 pint soufflé dish with butter. Put in the mixture, smooth it evenly and dot with butter. Cover the dish with foil and put into the preheated oven. Remove the foil after 20 minutes so that the potatoes get a good brown crust, and cook for a further 10-15 minutes.

Quark Soufflé Potatoes

8 floury potatoes, medium-sized

2oz butter, cut into pieces

4oz Quark (low fat soft cheese)

5 tablespoons light cream

4oz ham, diced

2 eggs, separated

1 tablespoon chives, chopped

salt & pepper

Wash and scrub the potatoes and bake them in their skins for about 40 minutes in a hot oven until soft. Cut off the top of each potato and scoop out the potato flesh with a teaspoon. Sieve the flesh and mix with the butter, Quark and cream; beat until smooth. Add the diced ham, the egg yolks and chives, and season with salt and pepper. Whisk egg whites until stiff and fold into the mixture. Refill potato skins with the mixture and bake at 180°C/350°F for 15 minutes. Serve very hot.

Pepper and Potato Bake

4 large tomatoes

2lbs potatoes, peeled and sliced paper-thin

salt & pepper

3 red or green peppers, seeded and cut into strips

2 cups Allgäu Emmentaler cheese, grated

1 cup light cream

2 tablespoons butter, cut into small pieces

Dip the tomatoes into boiling water for 2 minutes then skin them and cut into slices. Season the potato slices well with salt and pepper and put half into a buttered 2 pint soufflé dish. Add the peppers and grated cheese. Cover with remainder of the potatoes. Heat the cream (though not to boiling) and pour it over. Dot with the butter. Put into an oven preheated to 220°C/425°F and bake for about 1 hour on the lower shelf. Serve with green salad and fried Kassler (German smoked pork loin).

Rosti

$1\frac{1}{2}$lbs potatoes

salt & pepper

2 tablespoons butter

1 onion, peeled and finely chopped

2 tablespoons olive oil

Boil the potatoes in their skins in salted water for 15 minutes. Peel the potatoes and grate coarsely. Cut half the butter into flakes and add to the potatoes with the onion. Season with salt and pepper and mix lightly. Heat the olive oil and remaining butter in a heavy skillet. When hot add the potato mixture, pressing it lightly into a round cake. Fry over low heat for about 15 minutes until the underside is cooked, then turn the cake out on to a heated plate and quickly slip it straight back into the skillet. Fry gently on the other side for a further 10-15 minutes. Serve cut into wedges like a cake.

Meat Dumplings with Bok Choy

$\frac{1}{4}$ head bok choy

1 cup water or meat stock

2 tablespoons caraway seeds

1 bread roll

$1\frac{1}{2}$ cups ground beef

1 egg, beaten

1 tablespoon capers

salt & pepper

1 tablespoon toasted breadcrumbs

fat, for frying

1 tablespoon cornstarch

Cook the bok choy with the water or stock and caraway seeds for about 3 minutes. Set aside. Soak the bread roll in water for a few minutes then squeeze out the water. Mix the softened bread roll with ground beef, egg, capers, salt, pepper and breadcrumbs. Form the mixture into 4 balls and deep fry in hot fat until crisp and golden.

Drain the bok choy and combine liquid left in the pan with the cornstarch. Heat gently, stirring, then return the bok choy to the pan to warm through. Serve with the meat dumplings.

Chicken Dumplings

1 cup cubed roast chicken
2 tablespoons fresh parsley, chopped
½ onion, peeled and grated
½ teaspoon cayenne pepper
salt & pepper
½ teaspoon dried oregano
2 cups water
1 packet potato dumpling mix

Mix the chicken pieces with the parsley, onion, cayenne, salt, pepper and oregano. Pour the water over it. Make up the dumpling mix according to instructions, add the chicken mixture and allow to swell. Shape the dough into 8 dumplings with wet hands and cook for 10-15 minutes in boiling water.

Mushroom Croquettes

2lbs potatoes, peeled
2 cups flour
2 tablespoons butter
1 onion, peeled and chopped
5 cups mushrooms, peeled, washed and chopped
salt
1 teaspoon dried thyme
1 cup cold water
vegetable fat, for frying

Boil the potatoes in salted water until tender. Mash them and add the flour. Heat the butter in a skillet and fry the onions until softened. Add mushrooms and cook until the juices have evaporated. Season with salt and thyme and remove from the heat. Pour on the cold water, stir well and allow the mixture to cool. Knead the potato mixture briefly and combine with mushroom mixture, then shape it into croquettes about as thick as a thumb. Heat the fat in a skillet and shallow fry until golden and cooked through.

Jacket Potatoes with Cream Cheese Sauce

4 large potatoes
1 cup German double cream cheese
4 tablespoons light cream
1 small onion, peeled and finely chopped
1 clove of garlic, peeled and crushed
1 bunch fresh chives, chopped
salt

Wash the potatoes well and wrap in foil. Sprinkle a baking tray with salt and place the potatoes on the salt. Bake for 45 minutes in an oven preheated to 240°C/475°F. Mash the cream cheese and cream together with a fork until smooth. Add the finely chopped onions, garlic and chives and mix well.

When the potatoes are cooked, remove the foil, cut them open and spoon in the cream cheese sauce.

Saffron Potatoes

- 2 tablespoons olive oil
- 2 onions, peeled and finely chopped
- 2 leeks, finely sliced
- 2 fennel bulbs, finely sliced
- about 2 heaped teaspoons tomato purée
- 2 dried orange peel strips (preferably oven dried)
- salt
- freshly ground black pepper
- 3 cups hot water
- 1 lb firm potatoes, peeled and thinly sliced
- 2 carrots, washed, peeled and halved
- 2 garlic cloves, peeled and crushed
- celery salt
- pinch of saffron
- 2 hard-boiled eggs, shelled and sliced
- 2 tablespoons fresh parsley, finely chopped

Heat the oil in a large pan and quickly fry the onions, leeks and fennel. Add the tomato purée, orange peel strips, salt, pepper and hot water and stir. Add the potato slices, carrots and garlic. Season with celery salt and saffron. Cook the vegetables, uncovered, until they are quite soft. Remove and discard the carrots and orange peel. Drain the vegetables from the liquid and put the liquid to one side. Put the vegetables into a dish and decorate with the eggs and parsley. For the sauce, heat the reserved liquid again and boil rapidly to reduce, thickening further with extra tomato purée.

Lettuce and Dumpling Soufflé

- 2 cups ground beef
- 1 egg, beaten
- salt & pepper
- 1 teaspoon dried basil
- 1 teaspoon dried thyme
- 1 tablespoon fresh breadcrumbs
- 2 small iceberg lettuces, quartered
- 2 tomatoes, cut into eight pieces
- 1 cup white sauce
- 1 cup grated Allgäu Emmentaler cheese
- 1 egg yolk
- 1 oz butter, cut into small pieces

Mix the beef, egg, salt, pepper, basil, thyme and breadcrumbs together. Form the mixture into 1 inch dumplings. Cook the dumplings in boiling salted water for 15 minutes, then remove with a slotted spoon and drain. Put the lettuces, tomatoes and dumplings in the bottom of a large soufflé dish.

Mix the sauce with the cheese, egg yolk, salt and pepper. Pour this sauce over vegetables and dumplings and bake in an oven preheated to 200°C/400°F for about 20 minutes. Take the dish from the oven, dot the top with butter, return to the oven and bake until surface is lightly browned.

Potato Salad

- $1\frac{1}{4}$lbs potatoes
- salt
- 8 scallions, very finely chopped
- 1 small dill pickle
- 3 tablespoons vinaigrette dressing
- freshly ground black pepper

To garnish:

- fresh parsley, capers, pickles or hard-boiled eggs, as liked

Boil the potatoes in their skins in salted water until tender, then peel and allow to cool. Dice the potatoes and mix with the scallions, dill pickle, vinaigrette and black pepper in a salad bowl. Garnish with parsley, capers, pickles or hard-boiled eggs as liked, and serve.

Farmer's Breakfast

- $2\frac{1}{2}$lbs waxy potatoes
- 3oz fat bacon or German speck, cut into cubes
- 3 eggs
- 3 tablespoons milk
- salt
- $\frac{1}{2}$ cup cubed ham
- $\frac{1}{2}$ bunch fresh chives, chopped

Boil the potatoes in their skins, then peel them and allow to cool. Slice the cooled potatoes and fry with the bacon until golden brown. Whisk together the eggs, milk and salt. Add the cubed ham and chives and pour over the browned potatoes in the pan. Stir the mixture constantly until the eggs are firm then serve immediately.

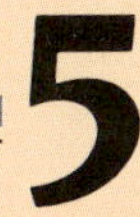

Vegetables and Salads

Traditionally the Germans eat a good deal of sauerkraut and few green vegetables. This is changing, and more vegetables and salads are served as side dishes nowadays.

Holstein Cheese Salad

Serves 2

- 6oz Tilsiter cheese, sliced
- ½ red bell pepper, cored, seeded and sliced
- ½ small cucumber, sliced
- 10 small radishes, sliced
- 1 small onion, peeled and sliced
- 6oz mixed pickles, chopped
- 1 tablespoon capers
- 4 tablespoons heavy cream
- soya sauce, to taste
- garlic powder
- salt & pepper
- chopped fresh chives, to garnish

Combine the cheese, bell pepper, cucumber, radishes, onions, mixed pickles and capers in a bowl. Mix the cream and soya sauce with garlic powder to taste and season with salt and pepper. Pour over the salad and leave to marinate for 1 hour. Serve garnished with finely chopped chives.

Sonthofen Salad

- 1 fennel bulb
- salt
- 2 sharp red-skinned eating apples
- ½ cup mayonnaise
- 2 tablespoons tomato catsup
- dash of Worcestershire sauce
- 1 tablespoon brandy
- 2 tablespoons light cream
- pepper
- 1 round lettuce, washed and dried
- 8oz ripe German Camembert, diced
- 2oz chopped walnuts

Clean the fennel bulb, chop it into small dice, and place immediately in a bowl of cold salted water to avoid discoloration. Quarter, core and slice the unpeeled apples directly into the bowl of cold water. Prepare a dressing by combining the mayonnaise, tomato catsup, Worcestershire sauce, brandy and cream, with salt and pepper to taste. Line 4 individual salad bowls with lettuce leaves, drain the fennel and apple slices and divide between the bowls, adding the cheese and walnuts at the same time. Pour some dressing over each bowl and serve.

Stuffed Cauliflower with Butter Sauce

- 1 cauliflower, washed, trimmed and left whole
- 1 tablespoon milk
- 9oz ground beef
- salt & pepper
- 2 teaspoons fresh thyme
- 1 egg, beaten
- ½ cup water
- 4 tablespoons wine vinegar
- 2 small onions, peeled and finely chopped
- 2oz butter
- 1 tablespoon light cream
- 2oz Quark (low fat soft cheese)

Boil the cauliflower for 10-15 minutes in salted water to which the milk has been added. Season the beef well with salt, pepper and thyme, and mix with the beaten egg to bind. Press the meat mixture into the hollow spaces between the cauliflower florets. Butter a large sheet of foil and wrap around the cauliflower to enclose completely. Bake in an oven preheated to 200°C/400°F for 50 minutes.

Meanwhile, heat the water, vinegar and onion together in a pan, and boil to reduce the liquid by two-thirds. Raise the heat and when boiling vigorously add the butter. When the butter has melted, add the cream and season with a little salt. Remove from the heat and quickly whisk the Quark into the sauce until it is foamy and light. Season the sauce to taste with pepper.

To serve, unwrap the cauliflower and cut horizontally into slices about ½ inch thick. Serve each slice topped with a spoonful of the butter sauce.

Stuffed Tomatoes

8 medium tomatoes, washed
salt & pepper
2 tablespoons white breadcrumbs
2oz butter
3oz fat bacon or German speck
1 onion, peeled and finely chopped
6oz ground beef
3oz Tilsiter cheese, diced

Cut off the tops of the tomatoes and keep on one side. Scoop the seeds out of each tomato and season the insides with salt and pepper. Line the inside of each tomato shell with breadcrumbs. Heat the butter in a skillet and fry the speck and onions until lightly browned. Add the ground beef, season with salt and pepper and fry for about 8 minutes, stirring constantly. Remove from the heat and stir in the diced cheese. Fill each tomato shell with this mixture. Replace the lids of the tomatoes and place them in a well buttered ovenproof dish. Cover and bake in an oven preheated to 165°C/325°F for 20 minutes. This dish can be served on its own, or with fried or broiled beef steaks.

Spring Salad

1 iceberg lettuce
½ cup fresh German cream cheese
4 tablespoons heavy cream
1 tablespoon oil
1-2 tablespoons lemon juice

salt
freshly ground black pepper
sugar
1 tablespoon fresh chives, chopped
6 hard-boiled eggs, peeled and quartered, to serve

Tear the lettuce into pieces. Combine the cream cheese, cream, oil and lemon juice with salt, pepper and sugar to taste and stir until smooth. Pour over the lettuce and sprinkle with the herbs and freshly ground pepper. Serve with the hard-boiled eggs.

Bavarian Cauliflower Cheese

1 cauliflower, about 2lbs, washed, trimmed and quartered

salt & pepper

2 tablespoons butter

2 tablespoons flour

$\frac{1}{2}$ cup milk

$\frac{1}{2}$lb processed cheese, cubed

1 egg yolk, beaten

grated nutmeg

juice of $\frac{1}{2}$ lemon, or to taste

4 slices white bread, toasted

butter, for toast

4 slices ham

4 tablespoons breadcrumbs

Wash cauliflower and break into florets. Boil in salted water for about 20 minutes until tender. Drain, reserving the water. Melt the butter in a heavy-based pan, add the flour and cook for 3 minutes, stirring constantly. Add the milk then $\frac{1}{2}$ cup of the cauliflower water, stirring constantly, then boil for about 2 minutes. Add the cheese and the egg yolk to the sauce and stir until melted and smooth. Season with salt, pepper, nutmeg and lemon juice to taste. Butter the slices of toast and use to line the bottom of a shallow ovenproof dish. Arrange the slices of ham on the toast and top with cooked cauliflower florets. Pour the sauce over, sprinkle with breadcrumbs and bake in a hot oven until golden brown on top.

Royal Bavarian Camembert Salad

mixed fresh herbs to taste, chopped

3 tablespoons oil

wine vinegar

4 German Camembert halves

2 dessert apples

½ celery head, cut into matchstick strips

1 bulb fennel, cut into matchstick strips

1 round lettuce, washed and dried

1 tablespoon chopped walnuts, plus a few walnut halves to garnish

Make a marinade by combining the wine vinegar with the oil and herbs. Add the cheese and leave for 2-3 hours. Quarter, core and slice the apples and mix with cheese slices, adding the chopped walnuts, celery and fennel. Line a salad bowl with a few lettuce leaves and tear the rest into small pieces. Combine with the other vegetables and put in the salad bowl. Garnish the salad with apple slices and walnut halves and serve.

Bok Choy with Beef

2 tablespoons oil

8oz beef fillet, cut into strips

salt & pepper

½ head bok choy, sliced

1 glass German white wine

4 tomatoes, peeled and cut into eighths

2 tablespoons soy sauce

Heat the oil in a large pan and fry the meat over a high heat until sealed. Add salt and pepper to taste and the bok choy. Cook for 5 minutes, stirring constantly. Reduce the heat, add the wine, cover the pan and cook for 20 minutes. Add the tomatoes and soy sauce and cook for a further 5 minutes.

Baden Potato and Carrot Purée

2 tablespoons oil

6 medium carrots, scrubbed and sliced

2 onions, peeled and chopped

½ cup water

2lbs potatoes, peeled and sliced

1 cup hot milk

2 tablespoons butter

salt & pepper

grated nutmeg

Heat the oil in a large pan and fry the carrots and onions until glossy. Add the water and cook, covered, for a few minutes over a low heat. Add the potatoes to the pan. Cook for a further 30 minutes until all the vegetables are soft, then purée in a blender or food processor. Gradually stir in the hot milk and butter, then season to taste with salt, pepper and nutmeg. Serve the purée with roast beef or pork or ground beef hash.

Beef Topped with Browned Cauliflower

1 large cauliflower, washed, trimmed and left whole

salt

9oz mixed ground beef

1 egg, beaten

1 onion, peeled and finely chopped

mustard

1 teaspoon dried marjoram

freshly ground white pepper

breadcrumbs

1oz butter

dried mixed herbs

Sauce:

1oz butter

3 tablespoons flour

1 cup hot stock

1 cup milk

salt

freshly ground white pepper

1 teaspoon ground caraway seeds

9oz Allgäu Emmentaler cheese, grated

1 egg yolk

Cook the cauliflower for 15 minutes in plenty of salted water. Remove from the pan and leave to drain. Mix the ground meat with the egg, onion, mustard and spices. Transfer to a skillet and fry gently for 10-15 minutes. Put into a fireproof dish. Divide the cauliflower into florets and arrange on top of the meat. Sprinkle with breadcrumbs, herbs and dot with the butter. Brown in an oven preheated to 220°C/425°F for 10 minutes.

Meanwhile, make the sauce. Melt the butter in a heavy-based pan, add the flour and cook for 3 minutes, stirring constantly. Add the hot stock and then the milk, stirring constantly. Season to taste with salt and pepper and stir in ground caraway seeds. Add the grated cheese and leave for 5 minutes to allow the cheese to melt. Beat the egg yolk in a bowl, add a little of the hot sauce and combine well, then pour the mixture back into the sauce which should be hot but *not* boiling. Taste and adjust seasoning if necessary. Serve the gratin with the sauce as soon as the sauce is ready.

Creamy Vegetables

Serves 2

10oz packet frozen summer vegetables, thawed

1 tablespoon fresh parsley, chopped

1 packet instant white sauce mix

$\frac{1}{2}$ cup water

$\frac{1}{2}$ cup light cream

1 egg yolk

grated nutmeg

pepper

Cook the vegetables according to the instructions on the packet. Drain well and sprinkle with the parsley. Make up the sauce mix using the water, cream and egg yolk, and season to taste with nutmeg and pepper. Serve with sausages and croquette potatoes.

Sausage Salad

1 iceberg lettuce

2 dessert apples

8oz Schinkenwurst (German ham sausage), cubed or sliced

6 tablespoons vinaigrette dressing

Tear lettuce into pieces. Quarter, core and slice the apples and combine with the lettuce and sausage. Pour the dressing over, toss well and serve.

Baden Wine-Grower's Supper

- 10oz Limburger or Romadur cheese, evenly sliced
- ½ cucumber
- 10oz Fleischwurst (meat sausage) or Lyoner sausage
- 3 tablespoons wine vinegar
- pinch of salt
- pinch of pepper
- pinch of sugar
- ½ teaspoon German mustard
- 3 tablespoons oil
- 1 onion, peeled and finely chopped
- mustard and cress or fresh parsley, to garnish

Cut the cucumber and the sausage in half lengthwise and slice each half crosswise. Combine the sliced cucumber and sausage in a serving bowl.

Make a dressing by combining the wine vinegar with the salt, pepper, sugar, mustard and oil. Taste and adjust the seasoning. Add the onion then pour the dressing over the salad and leave to marinate for 30 minutes. Just before serving garnish with mustard and cress or parsley.

Warm Sherried Chicken Salad

8 tablespoons oil

1 lb chicken breast fillets

2 tablespoons sherry

1 small apple

1 orange, peeled and segmented

1 iceberg lettuce, separated into leaves

3 tablespoons wine vinegar

½ teaspoon German mustard

salt, to taste

sugar, to taste

cayenne pepper, to taste

1 clove garlic, peeled and crushed

1 onion, peeled and finely chopped

Heat 2 tablespoons of the oil in a skillet and fry chicken breasts until light golden. Add the sherry and cook for a further 2-3 minutes. Remove and keep warm. Quarter, core and slice the apple and mix with the orange segments and lettuce leaves. Mix the wine vinegar with the remaining ingredients, including the rest of the oil, to make a dressing and pour over the lettuce, apples and oranges. Cut chicken breasts into small pieces and mix in. Serve.

Asparagus with Creamy Orange Sauce

3lbs asparagus spears, cleaned and peeled if necessary

pinch of salt

pinch of sugar

2 sticks butter plus a knob for boiling

3 egg yolks

freshly ground black pepper

1 tablespoon lemon juice

juice of 1 blood orange

Tie the asparagus into 3 bundles. Bring about 6 pints of water to the boil in a large pan and add the salt and sugar, and the knob of butter. Boil the asparagus for about 15-20 minutes until tender. Drain.

Meanwhile, melt the sticks of butter. Beat the egg yolks with salt, pepper and lemon juice in a bowl standing over a pan of simmering water until frothy. Take care not to let the mixture boil, otherwise the egg yolks will curdle. Fold the warmed butter slowly into the mixture, a little at a time, adding more butter once the previous amount has been completely absorbed. If the sauce should curdle, add a few drops of iced water and beat vigorously until smooth again. Whisk in the orange juice then serve immediately with the asparagus.

Ham and Onion Salad

1 iceberg lettuce

1 cup sliced ham, cubed

1 onion, peeled and chopped

4 tablespoons mayonnaise

1 tablespoon German mustard

1 tablespoon wine vinegar

salt & pepper

$\frac{1}{2}$ teaspoon mild paprika

2 tablespoons fresh dill, chopped

Remove and discard the outer leaves of the lettuce and tear the remaining leaves into small pieces. Mix all other ingredients together in a small bowl and pour over the lettuce.

'Fireland' Salad

1 iceberg lettuce

4 tablespoons mayonnaise

1 teaspoon German herb mustard

4 tablespoons soured cream

1 tablespoon fresh cream

1 tablespoon cranberry sauce

$\frac{1}{2}$ teaspoon salt

pinch of sugar

2 tablespoons lemon juice

Separate the lettuce leaves and place in a salad bowl. Mix all other ingredients together in a jug to form a smooth dressing and pour over the lettuce.

Gardeners' Soufflé

2¼lbs prepared fresh seasonal vegetables, cut into small pieces

2oz butter, softened

3 egg yolks

3 tablespoons grated cheese

salt & pepper

grated nutmeg

2 tablespoons flour

1 tablespoon lemon juice

1 cup vegetable stock or milk

5 egg whites

Preheat the oven to 230°C/450°F. Steam or boil the vegetables until slightly soft then drain. Cream the butter until soft and light, then add the egg yolks, cheese, salt, pepper, nutmeg and flour. Next add lemon juice and vegetable stock or milk. Beat the egg whites until stiff and fold in gently. Mix in the cooked vegetables and pour the mixture into a buttered 2 pint soufflé dish. Bake for about 45 minutes until well risen and browned. Serve immediately.

Chicken and Orange Salad

1 celery head

2 dessert apples

2 oranges, peeled, segmented and roughly chopped

scant 1 cup mayonnaise

10 walnuts, chopped

1 cup cooked chicken, roughly chopped

Madeira wine or sherry, to taste

lettuce leaves, to serve

Boil or steam the celery head whole until just soft, then cool slightly and cut into fine strips. Quarter, core and roughly chop the apples and stir into the mayonnaise with the oranges, walnuts, chicken and celery. Stir in a dash of Madeira wine or sherry, cover and chill for 1 hour. To serve, line a salad bowl with the lettuce leaves and spoon in the salad mixture.

Noodles with Broccoli and Hazelnuts

9oz tagliatelle (ribbon noodles)

salt

14oz prepared broccoli

1 stick butter

2oz hazelnuts, flaked

coarsely ground black pepper

2oz German Blue Cheese (Edelpilzkäse), coarsely chopped

Cook the tagliatelle in boiling salted water until 'al dente'. Drain. Cook the broccoli in the same way, then split up into florets. Drain. Melt the butter in a skillet and fry the nuts until golden, season with black pepper. Combine the drained hot noodles with the broccoli florets, hazelnuts and melted butter. Sprinkle the blue cheese over and serve immediately.

Desserts

With superb soft fruits and berries it's no wonder there's so many tempting desserts in the German recipe repertoire.

Patisserie Cream

- 2 cups milk
- 1 vanilla pod, split
- 2 egg yolks
- 1 whole egg
- 3oz sugar
- 2oz cornstarch
- 1oz butter

Bring milk to the boil, add the vanilla pod and leave to infuse in the milk for 10 minutes. Meanwhile beat the egg yolks, egg and sugar together in a bowl until thick, creamy and pale yellow in color. Sift the cornstarch into this and fold in gently. Bring the milk to the boil again, then remove the vanilla pod, scrape out the soft insides from the pod and mix these into the milk. Slowly pour the vanilla milk into the egg mixture. When smoothly blended, transfer to a heavy-based pan, place over a low heat and beat vigorously until it thickens. Allow the mixture to come to the boil, then pour into a bowl and allow to cool. To prevent a skin from forming spear a knob of butter on the end of a fork and smear over the surface.

Note:
Patisserie Cream can be used for filling in cakes, and desserts, and will keep for 2 days in the refrigerator.

Chocolate Charlotte

- about 14 sponge finger biscuits
- 1 quantity Patisserie Cream (see recipe)
- 2 sheets white gelatin
- $1\frac{1}{2}$ cups heavy cream
- 1 quantity Chocolate Mousse (see recipe page 133)
- 2oz chocolate, grated or flaked

Thickly butter charlotte mold and line with the sponge fingers. Prepare the Patisserie Cream as in the recipe, soak the gelatin leaves in water and dissolve in the Patisserie Cream while still hot. Whip 1 cup of the heavy cream until really stiff and fold into the cooled thickened Patisserie Cream. Pour into the charlotte mold and gently level the top. Chill for at least 2 hours in the fridge. Prepare the Chocolate Mousse and pour on to the set Patisserie Cream. Chill for a further 2 hours. To serve, trim the tops of the sponge fingers level with the top of the mousse, and invert the charlotte on to a flat plate, giving it a firm shake as you do so. Gently remove the mold. Whip the remaining cream until stiff and pipe rosettes over the charlotte. Sprinkle with the grated or flaked chocolate and chill until required.

Rote Grütze with Cream

4 cups raspberry or red currant juice, or cooked berry pulp

1 cup sugar

1 cup cornstarch

2 cups heavy cream

1 sachet vanilla sugar

Heat all but 2 tablespoons of the fruit juice or pulp with the sugar. Stir the cornstarch in the reserved juice and pour it into the hot juice, stirring well. Cook for about 5 minutes, stirring all the time. Rinse out a glass bowl with cold water, pour in the thickened fruit juice and allow to cool. To serve, turn it out on to a serving dish. Beat the cream with the vanilla sugar until stiff, then spoon on top of the Rote Grütze.

Chocolate Milk with Vanilla Ice Cream

4 cups milk

4 squares cooking chocolate

4 tablespoons sugar

8 scoops vanilla ice cream

chocolate flakes or curls, to decorate

Put half of the milk in a pan and heat gently. Melt the chocolate with the sugar in the hot milk, then stir in the remaining milk and whisk thoroughly. Put 2 scoops of vanilla ice cream into 4 individual glass dishes. Pour the chocolate milk over the top, sprinkle with chocolate flakes or curls and serve immediately.

Apple Butter Pastries

Pastry:

$4\frac{1}{2}$ cups flour

1 cup sugar

grated rind of 1 lemon

pinch of salt

3 egg yolks

3 sticks butter, chilled

Filling:

8 medium sized sharp dessert apples

juice of 1 lemon

1 cup flaked almonds

1 stick butter

$\frac{1}{2}$ cup sugar

1 teaspoon ground cloves

To make the pastry, heap the flour on a pastry board or work surface, make a well in the center and put the sugar, lemon rind, salt and egg yolks in it. Mix lightly with a little of the flour. Cut the chilled butter into pieces on to the flour and quickly knead the mixture into a smooth pastry. Chill in the refrigerator for 30 minutes. Roll out the pastry on a floured board thinly and place on a baking sheet. Peel, quarter, core and thinly slice the apples, sprinkling them with the lemon juice as you work. Cut the butter into pieces, and cover the pastry with it, along with the apple slices. Sprinkle the flaked almonds over the top. Mix sugar with the cloves and sprinkle over. Bake for about 20 minutes in an oven preheated to 220°C/425°F. Serve straight from the oven.

Bühl Plum Pudding

2lb plums, pitted and halved

2 cups water

1 cup sugar

grated rind of 2 lemons

10 sheets gelatin

4 tablespoons German plum brandy

ground cinnamon, to taste

2 sachets vanilla sugar

To decorate:

heavy cream

chopped almonds

Cook the plums in 1 cup of the water over a medium heat for 10-15 minutes, then purée them in a liquidizer. Put the purée with the sugar and lemon rind in a pan and heat until dissolved. Heat and dissolve the gelatin in the remaining water. Stir the plum brandy, cinnamon and vanilla sugar into the mixture. Rinse out a large pudding basin with cold water, pour in the mixture and chill in the refrigerator until firm. When ready to serve, turn the pudding out by immersing the basin briefly in warm water, then inverting it on to a plate, giving the basin a firm shake as you do so. To decorate, whip the cream stiffly and spoon or pipe over the pudding then sprinkle with the chopped almonds.

Fresh Pineapple with Raspberry Purée

serves 6

1 ripe pineapple

2 tablespoons brandy

4 tablespoons sugar syrup (made from 10oz white sugar boiled in 1 cup water until dissolved, then cooled)

9oz fresh or frozen and thawed raspberries

1 cup sugar

Peel the pineapple and slice into rounds about ¾ inch thick. Cut around the hard core in each slice with a sharp knife and remove. Lay the slices, overlapping, in a flat dish, pour the brandy and sugar syrup over and leave to marinate for about 1 hour. To make the raspberry purée, place the fruit and sugar in a blender or liquidizer and process until the sugar has completely dissolved. To serve, divide the pineapple slices between individual plates and pour some raspberry purée over each.

Fruit with Sabayon Sauce

2 tablespoons plum spirit or liqueur

4 tablespoons sugar syrup (made from 10oz white sugar boiled in 1 cup water until dissolved, then cooled)

1lb fresh fruit (strawberries, plums, grapes, kiwifruit etc) cleaned and chopped

4 egg yolks

2oz sugar

1 cup Marsala

Pour the plum spirit and the sugar syrup over the fruit and mix. Leave to stand for about an hour to allow the flavors to develop. Make the Sabayon sauce. Place the egg yolks and sugar in a heatproof bowl standing over a pan of hot water and beat until creamy and frothy. Add the Marsala, spoon by spoon, whisking all the time (keep the water in the pan just below simmering point). Spoon the fruit mixture into individual bowls and pour the lukewarm Sabayon sauce over it. Serve immediately.

Fried Ginger Apple Slices

3 medium sized crisp dessert apples

2 tablespoons lemon juice

2oz preserved ginger in syrup

3 tablespoons butter

3 tablespoons honey

Peel and core the apples and cut into rings, rubbing both sides of the apple slices with lemon juice as they are cut to avoid discoloration. Drain the ginger and cut into thin sticks or slices. Heat the butter in a skillet until frothy, and fry the apple rings for 5 minutes over a low heat. Spoon the honey, remaining lemon juice and the ginger over the slices and cook for a further 3 minutes. Serve hot.

Little Peter

- 2lb plums, pitted but left whole
- 1 cup sugar
- ½ a cinnamon stick
- 1 cup almonds
- 3 egg whites
- 4 squares chocolate, grated

Put the plums, with sugar to taste and cinnamon stick, in a pan and cook over a gentle heat for 5 minutes. Cool slightly then place 2 almonds in each plum and lay the plums in a buttered shallow fireproof dish. Beat the egg whites, beat in the remaining sugar, then fold in the grated chocolate and spread the mixture over the plums. Cook in an oven preheated to 200°C/400°F for about 20 minutes, until golden brown.

Apple, Lemon and Red Currant Purée

- 2½lbs cooking apples
- 1 cup German white wine
- 1 cup apple juice
- ½ a vanilla pod
- pared rind of 1 lemon
- 2 tablespoons red currants
- ½ cup water
- ¾ cup cornstarch
- about 2 tablespoons lemon juice
- heavy cream, for serving

Peel and core the apples, and cut into slices. Combine the wine, apple juice, vanilla pod, lemon peel and red currants in a pan, bring to the boil and poach apple slices gently for about 10 minutes until soft. Remove the vanilla pod and lemon peel. Stir the water into the cornstarch until smooth and add to the pan. Bring the mixture to a gentle boil, stirring until thickened. Add lemon juice to taste then pour into a glass dish and allow to cool. Serve with sweetened, lightly whipped cream.

Apple Pancakes

- 4 medium sharp dessert apples
- 2½ cups flour
- pinch of salt
- 3 eggs, separated
- 2 cups milk
- butter, for frying
- 2 tablespoons sugar
- pinch of ground cinnamon

Peel, core and thinly slice the apples. Sift the flour into a large bowl and mix with salt, egg yolks and milk to a smooth batter. Beat the egg whites until stiff and fold in with a metal spoon. Melt a teaspoon of butter in a skillet and when hot drop in a tablespoonful of batter. Fry lightly until the underside is brown, then turn the pancake carefully and cook on the other side. Continue until all the batter has been used up. To serve arrange apple slices over the top of each pancake as it is cooked and sprinkle with sugar and cinnamon.

Bilberry Pancakes

1 lb fresh bilberries, topped and tailed (or equivalent weight of drained, bottled or canned bilberries)

sugar, to taste

$2\frac{1}{2}$ cups plain flour

4 eggs, beaten

pinch of salt

3 tablespoons sugar

1 pint milk

2 tablespoons butter

Place the bilberries in a bowl. Add the sugar to taste and mix together. Sift the flour into a second bowl, make a well and place the eggs, salt and 3 tablespoons sugar in it. Stir together, starting in the center and gradually incorporate the flour, adding the milk at the same time. Beat for 2 minutes to form a thick batter. Fry the pancakes in a skillet, using a small knob of butter each time. As the second side of each pancake is cooked, cover it with bilberries and serve immediately.

Buttermilk Mold Pudding

4 cups buttermilk

1 sachet vanilla sugar

juice and grated rind of 1 lemon

10 sheets of gelatin

4 tablespoons hot water

1 liqueur glass Kirsch

To serve:

2 cups cleaned currants

$1\frac{1}{2}$ cups sugar

Combine the buttermilk, vanilla sugar, lemon peel and lemon juice in a large bowl (of at least 6 cups capacity) whisking thoroughly. Soften the gelatin in cold water, then dissolve it in the hot water. Stir the gelatin into the buttermilk mixture and combine well. Stir in the Kirsch. Rinse out a 2 pint pudding basin with cold water and pour in the mixture. Leave to set in the refrigerator. When ready to serve, turn out the pudding, sprinkle the currants with the sugar and serve alongside the pudding.

Trollinger Cherry Dessert

3 cups cherries, washed and stoned

2 cups Württemberger Trollinger (or other light red wine)

2 cups water

1 cup sugar

pared rind and juice of $\frac{1}{2}$ a lemon

pinch of ground cinnamon

3 tablespoons cornstarch

Wash and pit the cherries. Heat the wine with $1\frac{1}{2}$ cups of the water and the sugar, lemon peel and cinnamon. When the sugar has dissolved, add the cherries and cook for 5 minutes. Mix the cornstarch with the remaining $\frac{1}{2}$ cup of water, stir into the pan and cook for 3 minutes until thickened. Stir in the lemon juice. Allow to cool. Stir before serving.

Plum Cocktail

$1\frac{3}{4}$lb plums, pitted and halved

4 tablespoons confectioner's sugar

1 pot yoghurt

ground cinnamon, to taste

juice and grated rind of $\frac{1}{2}$ a lemon

3 small glasses dark rum or brandy

Purée the plums (reserving 4 halves for decoration) with the sugar in a liquidizer. Add the yoghurt, cinnamon, lemon juice and rind and the brandy. Pour the mixture into 4 cocktail dishes and serve, decorating each one with a plum half.

Fancy Shortbread

3 sticks German butter, plus extra for greasing

2 cups confectioner's sugar

5oz cornstarch

$1\frac{1}{2}$ cups milk

1 teaspoon salt

2 teaspoons grated lemon rind

5 cups flour, sifted

4oz chocolate, melted, for decoration

Beat the butter, confectioner's sugar and cornstarch together until smooth but not foamy. Add 1 cup of the milk. Then mix in the salt, lemon rind and flour. Knead until smooth. Add rest of milk only when dough is firm enough. Put the dough into a piping bag and pipe into decorative shapes on a greased baking sheet. Bake in an oven preheated to 190°C/375°F for about 10 minutes until light golden. Cool on a wire rack. Melt the chocolate in a heatproof bowl standing over a pan of hot water. Do not stir. Dip each shortbread in the melted chocolate and leave to dry on greaseproof paper.

Chocolate Mousse

8oz dark chocolate, broken into pieces

$\frac{1}{4}$ cup milk

$\frac{1}{4}$ cup heavy cream

4 egg yolks

3 egg whites

5oz confectioner's sugar

Melt the chocolate in a fireproof bowl standing over a pan of simmering water. Do not stir. Warm the milk in another pan and add melted chocolate, stirring to mix. Allow to cool. Mix the cream with the egg yolks and stir into the chocolate mixture. Whisk the egg whites with the sugar until stiff, then lightly fold into the chocolate cream mixture with a large metal spoon. Work quickly, being careful not to let the fluffy texture collapse, but do not leave any streaks of egg white in the mixture. Transfer to a serving bowl and chill for about 3 hours in the fridge, or use according to recipe instructions (see Chocolate Charlotte recipe).

Plum Soufflé

4 cups milk

5 cups fresh breadcrumbs

$\frac{1}{2}$ stick butter, melted

1 cup sugar

3 eggs, separated

1 teaspoon ground cinnamon

1 liqueur glass dark rum

2lb plums, pitted and halved

butter, for baking

Heat the milk and pour it over the breadcrumbs in a mixing bowl. Mix in the melted butter and sugar and allow to cool. Mix egg yolks, cinnamon, and rum together. Add the milk and breadcrumb mixture. Whisk the egg whites until stiff and fold into mixture. Spread half the mixture into a greased soufflé dish, then carefully place the plum halves on top. Spoon in the remaining mixture and dot with small pieces of butter. Bake for 60-70 minutes in an oven preheated to 200°C-220°C/400°F-425°F until well risen. Serve immediately.

Apricot Wine Soufflé

$1\frac{1}{2}$lbs apricots

1 cup water

1 cup sugar

grated rind of $\frac{1}{2}$ a lemon

$\frac{1}{2}$ cup German white wine

butter, for greasing

3 eggs, separated

1 tablespoon vanilla sugar

1 cup flour

1 teaspoon baking powder

confectioner's sugar, for sprinkling

Blanch the apricots for 1 minute in boiling water to cover, then quickly remove, slip off the skins and halve and stone the fruit. Combine half the sugar with the lemon rind and wine in an earthenware or ceramic bowl and marinate the apricot halves for 10 minutes. Drain carefully in a sieve. Grease an ovenproof dish and put the apricot halves in it. Beat the egg yolks with remaining sugar and vanilla sugar until creamy. Sift the flour with the baking powder and add this gradually to the yolk mixture. Whip the egg whites until stiff, and gently fold into the mixture. Spread it over the apricots, smooth the surface and cook for about 30 minutes in an oven preheated to 220°C/425°F, until well risen and golden. Sprinkle with confectioner's sugar and serve immediately.

Foamy Chocolate Quark in Pastry Flowers

Pastry:
2 eggs
3oz sugar
1 cup ground almonds
2 tablespoons flour
3 tablespoons butter
whole oranges, for shaping
Chocolate Quark:
1 egg, separated
2 tablespoons apricot jelly
8oz dark chocolate, grated
1 liqueur glass apricot liqueur
½ cup heavy cream
3oz confectioner's sugar
1 cup Quark (low fat soft cheese)

To make the pastry flowers, cream eggs and sugar together until light and frothy. Mix the ground almonds with the flour and work in 2 tablespoons of the butter. Use the remainder of the butter to grease 2 baking sheets. Place spoonfuls of the mixture on to the sheets and spread out into 6 inch circles. Bake at a medium heat (180°C/350°F) until light brown. While still hot, remove from the baking sheets with the help of a spatula and place each one over an orange. Gently pull into flower shapes. Leave for a few minutes to harden, then lift from the oranges, turn over and place in individual glass dishes.

To make the chocolate Quark, mix the egg yolk with the apricot jelly, 4 tablespoons of the grated chocolate and the liqueur in a large bowl. Whisk the cream until thick. Whisk the egg white until stiff then whisk in the confectioner's sugar. Fold the cream (keeping 2 tablespoons aside), the egg white and the liqueur mixture into the Quark. Spoon the whole mixture into the pastry flowers. Melt remaining chocolate in a heatproof bowl standing over a pan of hot water, stir in the reserved cream and pour decoratively over the Quark mixture in the pastry flowers.

Strawberry Ice Cream Cake

- 5 eggs, separated
- 5 tablespoons warm water
- 5oz sugar
- 1 tablespoon vanilla sugar
- 1oz confectioner's sugar
- 5oz plain flour
- 2oz cornstarch
- 1 teaspoon baking powder
- 1 pint strawberry ice cream
- 1 cup heavy cream
- chopped nuts, to decorate
- 10oz fresh strawberries

Beat the egg yolks with the warm water until frothy, add the sugar and vanilla sugar and beat until creamy. Whisk the egg whites with the confectioner's sugar until stiff, fold into the egg yolk mixture. Sift the flour, cornstarch and baking powder together and gently whisk in the egg mixture. Line a loose-bottomed cake tin with silicone paper and pour the sponge mix into it. Bake in an oven preheated to 180°C/350°F for about 30-35 minutes. Allow to cool slightly then remove the sponge from the tin and leave to cool on wire rack for 24 hours. Cut the sponge horizontally into three rounds. Sandwich ice cream between each layer and leave in freezer to set firm. Just before serving beat the cream until stiff. Cover the top and sides of the cake with cream and cover the sides with chopped nuts. Pile the strawberries on top and serve immediately.

Rumtopf

In May or June clean a large ceramic or earthenware pot which holds 10 pints liquid. During the year this will be filled with different, mainly soft, fruits. Use quality rum and only perfect fruits.

The first layers of a rumtopf always use the same equal quantities of sugar to fruit, later on half the amount of sugar to fruit is used.

JUNE

1lb strawberries: washed, dried and hulled; 8oz apricots: scalded in boiling water, peeled, halved or quartered, and stoned. Place in the pot. Cover with $1\frac{1}{2}$lb sugar and $1\frac{1}{2}$ 70cl bottles of rum. The rum should come 1 inch above the top of the fruit. Always cover pot with earthenware lid or cellophane and keep cool. Don't move the pot.

JULY

1lb raspberries: washed, hulled and drained. Place into the pot on top of the strawberries and apricots. Add 8oz sugar and pour in more rum (about $\frac{1}{2}$ bottle) to clear the fruit by about 1 inch.

AUGUST

1lb in total morello cherries; washed but unstoned and peaches and plums mixed: skinned by scalding them in boiling water, then halved or sliced and stoned. Cover fruit with 8oz sugar and $\frac{1}{4}$-$\frac{1}{2}$ bottle rum.

SEPTEMBER

1lb different plums: prepared as above. Add a further 8oz sugar and $\frac{1}{2}$ bottle rum.

OCTOBER

1lb ripe pears: peeled, cored and cut into small pieces. Pour in a further 8oz sugar and $\frac{1}{2}$ bottle rum.

Leave for several weeks, adding a further $\frac{1}{2}$ bottle rum. The fruits are good on top of ice cream, and the rum liquor can be mixed with sparkling wine.

Ice Cream Hearts

Serves 2

½ pint raspberry or cherry ice cream

2 tablespoons fresh fruit (or Rumtopf fruit, see recipe) chosen to complement ice cream (e.g. cherries with cherry ice cream)

2 liqueur glasses dark rum or fruit liqueur, for flambéing

Cut the ice cream into two thick slices, and trim into heart shapes. Place a tablespoon of fruit on top of each heart. Heat rum or liqueur in a ladle and carefully ignite with a match. Pour the flaming alcohol over the hearts and serve immediately. This is especially effective when the table is candle-lit.

Iced Melon

1 melon

9oz blackberries

1 liqueur glass blackberry liqueur

½ pint chocolate ice cream

½ pint cherry ice cream

Cut the top off the melon and cut the flesh into balls with a melon baller. Marinate blackberries in the liqueur for 1 hour. Just before serving, cut the ice creams into cubes and fill the melon with the blackberries, melon balls and ice cream cubes. Serve immediately.

Profiteroles with Fruit

6oz flour
pinch of salt
1 stick butter
½ pint water
4 eggs
8oz strawberries or raspberries
2oz sugar
1 liqueur glass orange liqueur
confectioner's sugar, to sprinkle

Sift the flour with the salt on to a sheet of greaseproof paper. Heat the butter with the water in a heavy-based pan until the butter melts. Raise the heat and bring the mixture to a rolling boil. Remove from the heat and immediately pour in all the flour. Beat with a wooden spoon until the dough is smooth and forms a ball which rolls cleanly off the sides of the pan. Cool slightly then beat in the eggs, one at a time; the dough should be shiny and thick enough to hold its shape but not stiff. Using a piping bag or two teaspoons, shape small mounds of dough on a baking sheet that has been greased or covered with silicone paper. Bake in an oven preheated to 200°C/400°F for 15-20 minutes until the profiteroles are well risen, golden and crisp.

Meanwhile, wash the fruit and put in a heavy-based pan with the sugar and liqueur. Simmer until the fruit is soft, then sieve the mixture into a clean pan and bring back to the boil over a low heat. Cook until the mixture has thickened into a thick purée, stirring occasionally. Leave to cool. To assemble the profiteroles, cut each bun in half, fill the bottom halves with purée, replace the tops and sprinkle with confectioner's sugar.

Snow Eggs

1 vanilla pod

2 pints milk

4 eggs, separated

7oz sugar

1oz confectioner's sugar

3 tablespoons butter

Halve the vanilla pod lengthwise and scoop out the middle into a small dish. Bring the milk to a boil and stir in half of the vanilla pod insides. Allow to cool slightly. Beat the egg yolks with 5oz of the sugar until light and creamy and slowly pour on the milk, stirring all the time. Whisk over a gentle heat until the sauce has thickened. Pour into a dish and leave to cool, stirring occasionally to prevent a skin from forming. Beat the egg whites with the remaining vanilla pod insides and the confectioner's sugar until stiff. Have ready a large pan of boiling water. Using two tablespoons drop egg-shaped dumplings of the mixture into the pan and boil for 5 minutes. Remove with a slotted spoon and transfer to the bowl containing the sauce. Heat the butter and remaining sugar together until caramel colored and pour over the egg whites to decorate. Serve at room temperature.

Imperial Pancakes

2 tablespoons raisins

2 tablespoons dark rum

4 egg yolks

3 tablespoons sugar

pinch of salt

4 cups milk

$\frac{1}{8}$ teaspoon vanilla essence

1 cup flour

5 egg whites

2oz butter

confectioner's sugar, for sprinkling

Macerate the raisins in the rum for at least 2 hours. Squeeze rum from raisins and reserve. Beat the egg yolks with the sugar and salt until thick and pale. Beat in the milk, vanilla essence and flour. Add the raisins. Beat the egg whites until stiff and fold in gently with a metal spoon. Melt 1 tablespoon of butter in a skillet. Put in half of the batter and cook over a low heat for 4 minutes until it rises and is slightly brown underneath. Slide on to a plate. Melt a further tablespoon of butter, return the pancake to the skillet, the other side up, and cook for a further 4 minutes. Divide the finished pancake into 6-8 pieces and put on a warmed plate. Then cook the second half of the batter in the same way. Melt the remaining butter in the skillet and return all the pancake pieces to the skillet. Cook for 2 minutes then dust with confectioner's sugar and serve.

Cream Caramel

Serves 6

2 cups milk

1 cup cream

1 vanilla pod, split

$1\frac{1}{2}$ cups sugar, plus 5oz for the caramel

4 whole eggs

2 egg yolks

Put the milk, cream and vanilla pod into a pan, bring slowly to the boil and simmer for 10 minutes. Meanwhile put the sugar for the caramel in another saucepan over a low heat and leave until melted and light brown in color (don't let it get too dark). Pour the caramel immediately into 6 individual ramekins and swirl it around so that the base and sides are thinly covered. Whisk the eggs and egg yolks with the remaining sugar until thick and foamy. Bring the milk back to the boil, then remove the vanilla pod, scrape the soft insides from the pod and mix these into the milk. Slowly pour the vanilla milk into the egg mixture, stirring constantly. Divide the mixture between the caramel-lined ramekin dishes and place the ramekins in a deep baking tin half-filled with hot water. Bake in an oven preheated to 180°C/350°F for 35 minutes until set. Cool and leave in refrigerator overnight. Turn out on to individual plates to serve. The caramel will have turned to liquid and will make a lovely light brown sauce.

Opposite page: *Top*, **Chocolate Mousse.** *Middle*, **Pears in Red Wine.** *Bottom*, **Cream Caramel.**

Chocolate Mocha Mousse

8oz dark chocolate, broken into pieces

5 eggs, separated

$\frac{1}{2}$ cup sugar

2 tablespoons extra strong black coffee

2 tablespoons mocha liqueur

1 cup heavy cream

grated chocolate, for decoration

Melt the chocolate in a fireproof bowl standing over a pan of simmering water. Do not stir. Beat the egg yolks with a third of the sugar until foamy. Whisk the egg whites until stiff. Stir the black coffee and mocha liqueur into the melted chocolate until silky and smooth. Stir in the egg yolk mixture, which should be lukewarm. Whip half the cream and carefully fold into the mixture, keeping as much volume as possible. Fold in the egg whites. Spoon the mousse into 4 dessert glasses or bowls and cover with foil. Leave to set in the refrigerator. Just before serving, whip the remaining cream, add the remaining sugar and use to decorate the mousse with the grated chocolate.

Pears in Red Wine

Serves 6

6 ripe unbruised pears

$\frac{1}{2}$ cup sugar

2 tablespoons lemon juice

6 peppercorns

1 clove

1 piece cinnamon stick

1 bay leaf

1 piece orange peel

2 cups red wine

Peel the pears, keeping the stalks on. Place the sugar, lemon juice, spices, orange peel and red wine in a pan. Arrange the pears, standing up, in the pan and simmer uncovered for about 20 minutes. Leave to cool in the liquid then chill. Transfer to a glass bowl and serve with cream.

Chocolate Bread Pudding

6oz butter

3 eggs

9oz wholegrain bread

3oz dark chocolate, grated

$\frac{1}{2}$ cup milk

juice of $\frac{1}{2}$ a lemon

Cream together the butter and the eggs. Crumble the bread into the mixture, add the grated chocolate, milk and lemon juice and mix to a dough. Pour into a greased 4 cup pudding basin or 8 inch ring mold and bake in an oven preheated to 180°C/350°F for 60-70 minutes, until pudding is firm. Serve hot with custard.

Variation:
To make the pudding extra special add dark rum to taste, or chopped brandy-soaked fruit to the dough before it is baked.

7

Cakes and Baking

Some of the most delicious cakes, pastries and gâteaux come from Germany. Often spiced, recipes also use a lot of delicious fresh fruit.

Poppyseed and Potato Cake

½lb potatoes, peeled, washed and grated
2 sticks butter
scant 1 cup sugar
1 packet vanilla sugar
8 eggs, separated
2oz chocolate, grated
1½ cups flour
1 teaspoon baking powder
1 pinch salt
½ cup milk
1 cup ground poppyseeds
To decorate:
10oz chocolate cake covering
small sugar flowers

Line a 10 inch springform tin with greaseproof paper. Add sufficient water to the potatoes just to cover. Cream the butter and beat in the sugar and the vanilla sugar. Beat in the egg yolks, one at a time. In a bowl add the grated chocolate.

Sieve the flour with the baking powder and salt. Add spoon by spoon to the creamed mixture, alternating with spoonfuls of the milk. Add the drained grated potato and ground poppyseeds and mix together. Whisk egg whites until stiff and fold in gently. Pour the mixture into the prepared tin and bake for 1 hour in a oven preheated to 180°C/350°F. Cool on a wire tray.

To decorate, melt the chocolate covering in a bowl standing over a pan of hot water and use to coat the cake. Decorate with small sugar flowers.

Chocolate Cakes

1 quantity German Sponge mixture (see recipe below)

breadcrumbs

5 squares dark chocolate

2oz butter

2 teaspoons redcurrant jelly

1 tablespoon coconut oil

¼ cup chopped almonds

Put the sponge mixture in a buttered 2 pint fireproof bowl lined with breadcrumbs. Bake for 30-40 minutes in an oven preheated to 180°C/350°F.

Cut the cooled cake into four layers. Break the chocolate into small pieces and melt it with the butter in a heatproof bowl standing over a pan of hot water and stir until smooth.

Spread the bottom of the cake with a quarter of the chocolate, put the second layer on top, spread this with 2 teaspoons redcurrant jelly and then a third of the remaining chocolate, put the third layer on top, then spread half of the remaining chocolate over and finally place the last layer on top.

For the topping warm the remaining chocolate with the coconut oil to give a good spreadable mixture. Cover the cake with this and sprinkle the chopped almonds on top.

German Sponge

Makes 2 cakes

2 eggs, separated

3 tablespoons warm water

½ cup sugar

1 sachet vanilla sugar

1½ cups flour

2 level teaspoons baking powder

1 tablespoon butter, melted

Butter a 8 inch cake pan and line with baking parchment. Beat the egg yolks with the water and gradually add two-thirds of the sugar and the vanilla sugar. Beat until smooth and creamy. Beat the egg whites until stiff and add the rest of the sugar gradually. Fold egg white into the egg yolk mixture. Sift the flour with the baking powder and fold into the mixture. Gradually add the melted cooled butter. Pour the mixture into the prepared pan and bake for 30-40 minutes in an oven preheated to 180°C/350°F.

Red Currant Kiss Cakes

1 cup confectioner's sugar, sifted

2 sticks butter

1 egg yolk

3 cups flour

8 egg whites

1½ cups sugar

4 cups prepared redcurrants

Mix the confectioner's sugar with the butter and egg yolk. Sift the flour into this and knead quickly to a smooth dough. Wrap in foil and chill in refrigerator for 1 hour. Roll the dough out to fit a 15x12 inch baking pan, and place it on the pan. Prick several times with a fork and bake for 12 minutes in an oven preheated to 220°C/425°F. Remove and allow to cool. Increase the oven temperature to 240°C/475°F. Beat the egg whites until stiff and gradually fold in the sugar. Fold in the redcurrants. Spread the mixture evenly over the par-cooked base, and cook for 10 minutes, keeping the oven door open a little during cooking. Allow to cool then cut the cake into portions and serve.

Potato Strudel with Apples

1lb potatoes, cooked and peeled

2½ cups flour

1 teaspoon baking powder

1 cup sugar

1 stick butter

1 small packet vanilla sugar

2 eggs

2½lbs apples

½ cup raisins

2 tablespoons sugar

1 teaspoon cinnamon

butter

Grate the potatoes and mix them with flour and baking powder. Add the sugar, butter, vanilla sugar and eggs. Knead this quickly into a firm dough, adding a little flour if dough becomes sticky. Peel, core and slice the apples. Roll the dough out and cover with sliced apples, raisins, sugar and cinnamon. Roll up, dot with butter and bake in an oven preheated to 200°C-220°C/400°F-425°F for 25-30 minutes until golden brown.

Coconut Drops

Makes about 36

- 2 sticks butter
- $\frac{1}{4}$ cup sugar
- $\frac{1}{2}$ cup honey
- 2 eggs
- 2 cups desiccated coconut
- 3 tablespoons grated orange rind
- $2\frac{1}{2}$ cups flour
- $\frac{1}{2}$ teaspoon baking powder
- $\frac{1}{4}$ teaspoon salt
- $\frac{1}{2}$ cup orange juice
- 2 squares cooking chocolate or cake covering

Beat $1\frac{1}{2}$ sticks of the butter until creamy. Gradually add the sugar, honey and eggs, stirring well between additions. Then fold in the coconut and grated orange rind. Sift the flour with the baking powder and salt and mix spoonfuls into the mixture alternately with spoonfuls of the orange juice. Place in well-spaced small mounds of 2 teaspoons each on a lightly greased baking tray and cook for 15 minutes in an oven preheated to 180°C/350°F.

Melt the chocolate but do not allow it to become hot. Mix remaining butter with chocolate and stir until the mixture is syrupy. Dip one half of each coconut drop into the mixture, then allow to cool and store in a dry place.

Rum Gugelhupf

3 sticks butter
1 cup sugar
6 eggs
$2\frac{1}{2}$ cups flour
$\frac{3}{4}$ cup cornstarch
1 packet baking powder
6 tablespoons dark rum
3 tablespoons lemon juice
2 tablespoons orange juice
grated rind of 1 lemon
2-3 tablespoons fresh breadcrumbs
$1\frac{1}{2}$ cups confectioner's sugar, sifted
2 tablespoons toasted flaked almonds
confectioner's sugar

For the dough, cream 1 stick of butter with the sugar until light and fluffy. Stir in 5 of the eggs, one at a time. Sift the flour, cornstarch and baking powder together and fold in. Finally add 5 tablespoons of the rum, 2 tablespoons of the lemon juice, the orange juice and half the grated lemon rind. Butter a gugelhupf tin and sprinkle the breadcrumbs over the inside. Pour the mixture into the mold and bake for 60-70 minutes in an oven preheated to 190°C/375°F. Turn out on to a baking tray and allow to cool.

For the butter cream, beat the remaining cup of butter until creamy, and stir in the confectioner's sugar, remaining egg and, drop by drop, the remaining 1 tablespoon rum and 1 tablespoon lemon juice. Add the remaining grated lemon rind to taste. Cut the cooled gugelhupf horizontally into 2 layers and sandwich the layers back together with butter cream. Press the flaked almonds into the butter cream edges. If desired dust with confectioner's sugar.

Rum Savarin with Red Currants

Serves 8-10

Savarins:
$3\frac{1}{2}$ cups flour
1 oz fresh yeast
$\frac{1}{2}$ cup lukewarm milk
$1\frac{1}{2}$ sticks butter
3 tablespoons sugar
$\frac{1}{2}$ teaspoon salt
$\frac{1}{2}$ teaspoon grated lemon rind
4 eggs, beaten

Filling:
2 cups sugar
2 cups hot water
4 tablespoons white rum
1 cup red wine
1 tablespoon sugar
juice of 1 orange
5 cups prepared red currants

To garnish:
1 cup heavy cream
1 tablespoon pistachio nuts

To make the savarins, sift the flour into a bowl, and make a well in the center. Dissolve the yeast in the milk and mix into the flour. Cover with a cloth and leave in a warm place for 15 minutes. Melt the butter, add 2 tablespoons of the sugar, the salt, lemon rind and eggs and mix briefly. The mixture should not become foamy. When the yeast and flour show cracks on the surface, add the egg mixture and beat well to give a smooth dough that pulls easily and is not too firm. Allow to stand for a further 15 minutes. Grease two 6 inch savarin rings with butter, dust with flour and half-fill with dough. Cover with a cloth and again allow to stand until doubled in bulk (about 15 minutes). Bake for 25-30 minutes in an oven preheated to 220°C/425°F, then remove from the tins and place on a wire rack.

Make the filling. Dissolve the sugar in the water and then add the rum. Spoon this syrup over the savarins, allowing the excess to drain off. Heat the red wine with the sugar and orange juice and poach the redcurrants until soft. Fill the hot savarins with this mixture, garnish with whipped cream, sprinkle with pistachio nuts and serve.

Pepperthalers

2 sticks butter
$\frac{1}{2}$ cup sugar
1 egg yolk
1 tablespoon grated orange rind
1 tablespoon grated lemon rind
$\frac{1}{2}$ cup chopped candied fruit or fruit peel
$\frac{1}{2}$ cup ground almonds
$\frac{1}{2}$ cup honey
4 cups flour
1 teaspoon baking powder
$\frac{1}{4}$ teaspoon bicarbonate of soda
$\frac{1}{2}$ teaspoon salt
$\frac{1}{8}$ teaspoon freshly ground black pepper
$\frac{1}{8}$ teaspoon ground nutmeg
$\frac{1}{4}$ teaspoon ground cinnamon
$\frac{1}{4}$ teaspoon ground cloves
1 teaspoon aniseed
$\frac{1}{2}$ cup brandy
2 tablespoons lemon juice
$1\frac{1}{2}$ cups confectioner's sugar
3 tablespoons water

Cream the butter and gradually add the sugar, beating until light and fluffy. Add the egg yolk, orange and lemon rind, candied fruit, almonds and honey and mix well. Mix the flour with the baking powder, bicarbonate of soda, salt, pepper and spices, sieve it and add to the mixture with the brandy plus lemon juice, in alternate spoonfuls.

Place teaspoonfuls of the mixture on a greased baking sheet and bake in an oven preheated to 180°C/350°F for 15 minutes or until lightly browned.

Meanwhile mix the confectioner's sugar with the water to make a smooth glaze. Pour this over the pepperthalers as soon as they come out of the oven, then put them back into the oven for a further 2 minutes.

Marzipan Cherry Cake

12 egg yolks
$1\frac{1}{2}$ cups sugar
1 cup ground almonds
$\frac{1}{2}$ vanilla pod, soft insides removed and shell discarded
2oz butter
6 egg whites, whisked
1 cup flour
$\frac{1}{2}$ cup Graham Cracker crumbs
10oz cherry jam
2 tablespoons Kirsch
2 tablespoons sugar syrup, plus extra for decorating
1lb marzipan, soft textured
$\frac{1}{2}$ cup sugar
1 cup roasted, flaked almonds

Line a 10 inch springform tin. Mix together 6 of the egg yolks with one third of the sugar, all ground almonds and soft insides of vanilla pod, and beat vigorously until increased in volume. Melt the butter and add gently to the mixture. Whisk the egg whites and fold in the remaining sugar. Mix together the flour and cracker crumbs and add to almond mixture, folding in the whisked egg whites at the same time. Place the mixture in the prepared tin. Bake for 35-40 minutes in an oven preheated to 190°C/375°F. When cooked, remove from the oven and leave to cool overnight.

Cut the cake horizontally into three rounds. Mix together the cherry jam, Kirsch and 2 tablespoons of the sugar syrup and spread each layer with one quarter of the mixture, reserving the remainder. Place the cake rounds on top of each other. Mix the marzipan with the $\frac{1}{2}$ cup sugar and work in the remaining 6 egg yolks, one at a time.

Put two-thirds of the marzipan mixture into a piping bag fitted with a star nozzle. Thin the remaining marzipan with a little sugar syrup and use to coat the top and sides of the cake. Press the toasted flaked almonds to the sides of the cake. Pipe the marzipan on the top of the cake as illustrated then brown the top under a preheated broiler. Using reserved jam, pour a little into spaces between the piped marzipan.

Fruit Slices

1 quantity, German sponge mixture (see recipe page 144)

about 1lb fresh fruit, to choice

2 tablespoons sugar

2 cups heavy cream, whipped

flaked almonds (optional)

Sprinkle the fresh fruit with the sugar. Spread half the whipped cream over the sponge to insulate it from the fruit juices. Cut the cake into about 8 pieces and cover each piece with fruit. Finally decorate with remaining whipped cream and/or flaked almonds.

Vanilla Crescents

7oz butter

$\frac{1}{2}$ cup sugar

insides of $\frac{1}{2}$ vanilla pod

4oz ground almonds

2 cups flour, sifted

2oz sugar

1 sachet vanilla sugar

Cream the butter and $\frac{1}{2}$ cup sugar until smooth, then beat in the insides of the vanilla pod and the almonds. Add the sieved flour, knead well and chill for 1 hour. Shape the dough in a roll 1 inch in diameter and cut into slices 1 inch thick. Shape these into small crescents and arrange on a baking sheet. Bake for 8-10 minutes in an oven preheated to 190°C/375°F. Meanwhile mix the remaining sugar with vanilla sugar. When the crescents are cooked, remove from the oven, cool slightly then roll in the sugar.

Rhine Cinnamon Wafers

$1\frac{1}{2}$ sticks butter

$\frac{3}{4}$ cup sugar

1 sachet vanilla sugar

3 eggs, separated

$1\frac{1}{2}$ cups flour

2 teaspoons cinnamon

1 teaspoon ground ginger

1 teaspoon baking powder

$\frac{1}{2}$ teaspoon salt

2 pints soured milk

1 bacon rind, for greasing

1 cup apple sauce

5 squares melted chocolate

Beat the butter until creamy then gradually add the sugar and vanilla sugar and beat until foamy. Mix the egg yolks thoroughly into the butter mixture. Mix the flour, with the cinnamon, ginger, baking powder and salt. Sift, then mix in spoonfuls into the dough, alternating with spoonfuls of the soured milk. Beat the egg whites until stiff and fold into the mixture. Pour in portions on to a greased wafer plate and cook until pale golden. While still hot pull into a cone shape over a thick spoon handle. (If no wafer plate is available, the dough can be baked in a waffle iron.) Serve warm, either filled with apple sauce, or with melted chocolate poured over them.

Cookies for Wine

3 tablespoons German white wine
3 tablespoons soured cream
3 tablespoons sugar
2 tablespoons Kirsch
3 egg yolks
plain flour (see method)
butter (see method)
1 egg white, lightly beaten
sugar, for sprinkling

Work all the first five ingredients together with enough flour to make a firm dough. Weigh the dough and add half its weight in butter. Knead quickly into the pastry, wrap in foil, and chill overnight in the refrigerator.

The next day, roll the dough out on a floured board until about $\frac{1}{4}$ inch thick. Cut into small shapes (squares, rounds, stars, hearts etc.), with a cocktail cutter. Brush with beaten egg white and sprinkle with a little sugar. Bake in an oven preheated to 200°C/400°F for about 15-20 minutes until pale golden (*not* brown). The cookies should not be too sweet, and are delicious served with wine.

Black Forest Gâteau

8oz dark chocolate, at room temperature
15oz jar of German sour cherries
3-4 tablespoons Kirsch
2 cups heavy cream
2 tablespoons half-and-half
3 ready made chocolate sponge cakes, 9 inches in diameter
fresh cherries, to decorate

Using a potato peeler 'shave' the block of chocolate into thin curls. Chill. Drain the syrup from the cherries and mix with the Kirsch. Whisk the cream with the half-and-half until stiff. Place one of the cakes on a serving plate and prick several times with a skewer. Sprinkle half of the cherry juice over, then spread a quarter of the cream over and arrange half the sour cherries on top, leaving a 1 inch margin around the sides. Place the second cake layer on top, sprinkle with the remaining cherry juice, spread a quarter more cream over, and arrange the remaining sour cherries on top. Position the third cake on top and press down lightly. Cover the top and sides of the cake with cream, and spoon chocolate curls over the top, leaving a gap in the center. Fill the center with fresh cherries and more chocolate. Chill for 1-2 hours before serving.

Apple Pudding with Orange Cream

3lb apples

$\frac{1}{2}$ pint orange juice

brown wholemeal bread, thinly sliced, enough to line dish

1 stick butter, melted

To serve:

1 cup heavy cream

1 liqueur glass orange liqueur

Peel and quarter the apples. Place in a pan with the orange juice and bring to the boil. Simmer, uncovered, until the liquid has reduced, then allow to cool. Dip the slices of bread in melted butter and use to line a 2 pint fireproof dish. Spoon the apples in the middle and cover with more slices of bread. Bake the pudding on the bottom shelf of an oven preheated to 165°C/325°F for $1\frac{1}{2}$ hours.

To serve, whip the cream with the orange liqueur until stiff. Turn the pudding out on to a plate and serve hot with the orange cream.

Colorful Cookies

Cookies:

5oz confectioner's sugar

7oz butter

1 egg yolk

grated rind of $\frac{1}{2}$ a lemon

1 teaspoon salt

3 cups flour, sifted

8oz black currant jelly

To decorate:

melted chocolate

frosting (made from 4oz confectioner's sugar combined with 1-2 tablespoons hot water)

flaked almonds

pistachio nuts

hundreds and thousands

Work the confectioner's sugar into the butter until smooth, then add the egg yolk, lemon rind and salt and knead in the flour to achieve a smooth pastry. Roll into a ball and leave, covered, in a cool place for 1-2 hours. Roll the pastry out until $1\frac{1}{2}$ inch thick and cut out into biscuit shapes. Place on a baking tray and bake for 8-10 minutes in an oven preheated to 190°C/375°F. Cool on a wire tray. To finish slightly warm the blackcurrant jelly and spread over the bottom side of half of the biscuits, then sandwich the biscuits together in pairs.

Decorate the biscuits by sprinkling the tops with confectioner's sugar, spreading them with melted chocolate or frosting and then arranging sliced almonds, pistachios and hundreds and thousands on top.

Chocolate Gâteau

5 eggs, separated
5 tablespoons hot water
1 cup sugar
$2\frac{1}{2}$ cups plain flour
2 level teaspoons baking powder
4oz grated dark chocolate
dark rum, for sprinkling
2 cups heavy cream (or 1 cup light cream plus 1 cup heavy cream)
chocolate flakes, to decorate

Beat the egg yolks with the hot water and sugar until thick and creamy. Whisk egg whites until they form stiff peaks and fold into the mixture. Sift together the flour and baking powder and add to the mixture with the grated chocolate. Blend very lightly with a whisk and pour into a 9 inch loose-bottomed cake pan. Bake in an oven preheated to 180°C/350°F until golden brown. Cool on a wire rack.

Slice the cake horizontally into three rounds and sprinkle each layer with rum. Whip the cream until stiff and spread one quarter over each round. Place the three rounds on top of each other and spread some of the remaining cream over the gâteau sides, reserving a little to pipe decorations on top. Decorate with chocolate flakes and serve.

Original Prince Regent Cake

4 sticks butter
$1\frac{1}{2}$ cups sugar
5 eggs, plus 4 yolks
1 cup flour
1 cup potato flour
grated rind of $\frac{1}{2}$ a lemon
3 tablespoons of rum
4 egg yolks
4 squares dark chocolate
2 tablespoons mocha
1 teaspoon rum
5 squares cooking chocolate or chocolate cake covering
1 cup apricot jelly, softened
crystallized violet petals, optional

Beat 2 of the sticks of butter until creamy and gradually cream in half the sugar. Stir in 2 of the whole eggs. Separate the remaining 3 whole eggs and add the yolks to the mixture, one at a time. Sift the flour with the potato flour, mix with the grated lemon rind and mix in the rum, a spoonful at a time. Finally beat the three egg whites with $\frac{1}{2}$ cup of sugar until stiff and fold into the mixture. Preheat the oven to 190°C/375°F and grease and flour an 8 inch cake pan. Make 6-8 cakes from the mixture, using 2 tablespoons of mixture each time and baking them for 6-8 minutes until light brown. Cool on a baking tray. Reduce the oven temperature to 180°C/350°F.

Dissolve remaining $\frac{1}{2}$ cup sugar in $\frac{1}{2}$ cup water over a low heat, then increase the heat and boil the syrup until the thread stage is reached (11°C). Whisk the 4 egg yolks until frothy. Add the hot syrup to the eggs, beating continuously. Continue beating until the mixture is cool and thick. Add remaining 2 sticks butter in small pieces. Melt the plain dessert chocolate with the mocha and rum in a heatproof bowl standing over a pan of hot water and add to the mixture.

Spread the cooled cake with this chocolate butter cream and sandwich together. If the cream is too soft, put the cake in the refrigerator until it has firmed up. Prepare a chocolate glaze by dissolving $\frac{1}{2}$ cup sugar with $\frac{1}{2}$ cup water over a low heat, then boil the syrup until thread stage is reached. Meanwhile melt the cooking chocolate in a heatproof bowl standing over a pan of simmering water. Combine the syrup with the chocolate and stir continuously until the glaze has cooled a little. Brush the cake with softened apricot jelly. Spread the glaze over the cake and return to the oven for 1 minute.

Strawberry Cream Roll

- 5 eggs, separated
- 3 tablespoons water
- 9oz sugar
- 1 sachet vanilla sugar
- 1 cup plain flour
- 3oz cornstarch
- 1 level teaspoon baking powder
- 2 cups heavy cream
- $1\frac{1}{2}$lb strawberries, halved or quartered
- confectioner's sugar, for dusting

Whisk the egg whites with the water until stiff, then whisk in 7oz of the sugar, a little at a time. In another bowl mix the vanilla sugar with the egg yolks, plain flour, cornstarch and baking powder. Fold in the egg white mixture. Line a swiss roll pan with buttered baking parchment or non-stick silicone paper. Spread mixture over pan. Bake in an oven preheated to 180°C/350°F until golden brown, then turn out on to a damp cloth. Leave to cool. Beat the cream with the remaining sugar until stiff then spread over the cooled sponge. Lay the strawberries over the cream layer then roll the sponge up with the help of the cloth. Dust with confectioner's sugar and serve.

Stollen

1oz fresh yeast
2 tablespoons warm water
3oz confectioner's sugar
pinch of salt
6 tablespoons warmed milk
2 tablespoons dark rum
few drops of almond essence
4 cups plain flour
1 egg, beaten
5oz butter, softened
2oz raisins
2oz candied cherries, chopped
1oz currants
1oz chopped angelica
2½oz cut mixed candied peel
1½oz flaked almonds
confectioner's sugar, for dredging

Mix the yeast with the water. Dissolve 2oz of the confectioner's sugar and the salt in the milk. Add the rum, almond essence and yeast liquid. Put the flour in a large mixing bowl and make a well in the center. Add the yeast mixture, egg and 3oz of the butter, cut into pieces. Add to this the raisins, cherries, currants, angelica, mixed peel and almonds. Mix to a soft dough then knead for 10 minutes. Leave to rise in a warm place until doubled in size. Knead again, then roll out into a rectangle measuring 12x8 inches. Melt the remaining butter and brush over the dough, then sprinkle with the remaining confectioner's sugar. Fold in the two long edges to overlap at the top, then press together lightly and taper the ends. Place on a greased baking sheet, brush with the remaining melted butter and leave in a warm place until doubled in size. Bake in an oven preheated to 190°C/375°F for about 45 minutes. Cool and dredge with confectioner's sugar.

Christmas Tree Decorations

Makes 25-30

1½ cups sugar
½ cup honey
5oz coconut cream
5 cups flour, sifted
2 heaped tablespoons cocoa or powdered drinking chocolate
1 tablespoon ground ginger
1 teaspoon ground cinnamon
1 egg
¼oz potash (from a drugstore)
1 tablespoon rosewater or water
To decorate:
½ cup confectioner's sugar
1 egg white
food colorings
colored balls
hundreds and thousands

Place the sugar, honey and coconut cream into a pan and stir over a gentle heat until the sugar has dissolved. Cool. Mix the flour with the cocoa and the spices in a large mixing bowl. Add the cooled sugar mixture, the beaten egg and the potash mixed with the rosewater. Knead into a dough and roll out on a floured board until ¼ inch thick. Cut into shapes and place on a greased baking sheet. Bake in an oven preheated to 200°C/400°F for 12-15 minutes. Cool on a wire tray.

To decorate, prepare a frosting by mixing the confectioner's sugar with the egg white and tint all or part of it with food colorings, as liked. Frost each biscuit, then decorate further with colored balls and hundreds and thousands, as liked.

Strawberry and Kirsch Meringue

6 egg whites
10oz sugar
2 teaspoons cornstarch
insides of ½ vanilla pod
pinch of salt
1lb strawberries, hulled and halved
2 tablespoons Kirsch
1 cup heavy cream
1 tablespoon confectioner's sugar

Draw a 7 inch circle on a sheet of greaseproof paper and lay on a baking sheet. Whisk the egg whites until stiff, then slowly whisk in the sugar, cornstarch, vanilla and salt. Put the mixture into a piping bag fitted with a plain nozzle and pipe into a round on the baking sheet, following the outline of the circle, then pipe another ring around the edge of the meringue to make a 'wall'. Bake in an oven preheated to 140°C/275°F for 3-4 hours, leaving the oven door slightly open (if the meringue browns, reduce the heat). Remove and allow to cool. Cover the cooled meringue with the strawberries and sprinkle with Kirsch. Beat cream with the confectioner's sugar until stiff, and pipe over the strawberries. Serve immediately.

Index

PICTURE CREDITS

Creative Cartography — Map P.7

Erroll Watson — Black and white line drawings